and after

Photographs Tom Bryan

For Eleanor,

THE
GLORY
of the
GARDEN
and the Cycle of
the Year~

Handwritten and illustrated
by the author

Joan Wolfenden

Joan Wolfenden

By the same author:

The Peacock Vane Cookery Book: RECIPES TO RELISH

First published in Great Britain by Peacock Vane, Bonchurch Isle of Wight
Copyright © Joan Wolfenden 1982

Acknowledgement is made, with thanks, for the extract from Henry de vere Stacpoole's "In a Bonchurch Garden" published by Hutchinson in 1937 ~ ~

ISBN 0 9506749 1 5

Produced by Crossprint, Newport, Isle of Wight
Printed in Singapore

For Frankie & David with love

BONCHURCH GARDENER

When you come to think on it
   Religion's much like weeding.
    The little annual petty sins
    Don't take a lot of heeding —
    Then there's the bigger, strong ones;
    You got to stop them seeding.

But when it comes to butterbur
   Why, that's a proper bastard!
    I reckon Rector's right to say
    Old Nick — he be a dastard.
    You cut it down & pulls it Monday
    'Tis waxing twice as strong come Sunday!

Deep roots: dandelion, oxalis and dock,
   When you've handled that lot
    You've still to fight the rock!

3

INTRODUCTION

This book about my flowers and garden was begun on 1st January, 1981 and I hope it will be finished on 31st December, 1981. Every morning I tip out of bed into the garden, garbed in scruffy clothes to fight the weeds and the wind, the snails, slugs and other pests. After a couple of hours I pack up, pick the most beautiful bloom I can find and put it into a specimen vase and place it at the foot of the cedarwood stairs which lead up to my studio. The cedar tree died of old age. After weathering for two years it was cut into planks and made me a studio in a wasted space in the roof — stairs, floor, walls and a splendid sky-light and french windows out to the very topmost crag of the cliff. Then comes the blessed relief of a wallow in the bath, fresh raiment, an early brunch, forty winks, a second cup of "early morning tea" and up those stairs!

My garden is on a cliff looking south to the Channel over a bowl of forest trees, beech and

4

lime mostly.   There is a cedar, a monkey puzzle
and a macrocarpa in the distance and, alas, the elms
are no more.

The flowers must be painted first and then the
words fitted on to the page.   Most thoughts come to me
when weeding and many's the muddy note that gets jotted
down.

It was Henry de vere Stacpoole's garden ~ he bought
it after writing The Blue Lagoon which sold over one
million copies. Here is a little extract of his description.
(The Island has never had grey squirrels. The few we have
are our native red.)

From: In a Bonchurch Garden.   1937.
"This garden, though supposed to be cultivated,
is wild at heart.
It is mostly trees and rocks: to explore it all
comfortably one would want to be a goat because of
the steepness of the slope on which it is set. But there
is a lawn with an "herbaceous border" so trimly kept
that people, deluded by it and looking down hill at
the goatpaths and shrub tops and little dells, palm tree

fronds, and the yellow tint of wattle, sometimes ask how many gardeners I keep.

I keep only one. That is to say I pay for one. But there are others, seen and unseen, who work unpaid in this old Victorian wilderness of a garden that seems to me sometimes haunted by fairies at night and sometimes, in sub-tropical noons of summer, by Victorian shades, gentlemen in shepherd's plaid trousers and with whiskers, ladies with parasols leading children wearing pantalettes ~ people who were all here once and whose gardening activities still remain in evidence.

That Mediterranean heath, reckoned the tallest in England did not take a ticket and travel from Marseilles to adorn of its own free will a Bonchurch garden. No, it and its travelling expenses were paid for with British gold taken out of British breeches pocket belonging to the days that are no more. ~ ~ ~

Squirrels plant trees; they may be ranked as invisible gardeners; they don't carry rakes or watering cans, and one hasn't to lick their insurance stamps, and no inspector ever comes to ask me how many squirrels I employ; still they are there, doing their stuff, as the Americans say.

There are quite a number of trees here planted by nuthiding squirrels, and no doubt they have other jobs to do as well. ~ ~ ~

Which brings me to the hour of sunset. Not the sunset before me, as I sit writing, that looks over the high downs at the blushing Culver Cliffs and the blue of Sandown Bay. but the sunset of a gracious and leisurely age that has all but passed, whose light still lingers in this garden and the other gardens of Bonchurch. ~ ~ ~ "

When I took it on some fifteen years past it was a wilderness. Now I hope it is restored to some of its old splendour. At the minute a local boy and I are digging a pool at the foot of the cliff. I have a little one at the top and I hope next year to have a waterfall and bog-plants growing down the cliff. That's the fun of a garden, thinking of next year and dipping into those shiny catalogues of hope and promise.

Every picture is painted from life at the time of the month in the journal. Each illustration is life size ~ scaled down a little by the printers ~ which, I hope, will make it easier, especially for the less experienced, to identify the plants.

7

At the back there is an index to show you your way about the book. Following this introduction is a list of what can be planted so that there is always some plant at its best throughout each week of the year ~ a flower or a shrub displaying against the lawns, the rocks and the sky.

I do hope that you will enjoy my year's labour both in the garden and in the studio.

PLANTING LIST

The shrub of the month is in block capitals. There are hundreds more to choose from. The ones I give are the ones I grow. In a small garden the twelve in block capitals should give pleasure the year round Then there are another fifty-two in italics. These are my favourite flowers of the week.

Finally I add some more flowers that I enjoy Obviously the size of your garden must determine the number of plants you may grow.

JANUARY
MAHONIA JAPONICA
Jasmine nudiflorum
Iris stylosa
Bergenia
Viburnum laurestinius

Iris stylosa	Salix vitellina
Viola odorata	britzensis (red
Snowdrop	darked form of golden

FEBRUARY
FORSYTHIA
Garrya elliptica
Chaenomeles superba
Flowering currant
Hazel

Iris reticulata
Pussy willow	Aubretia	Daffodil
Coronilla	Alyssum saxatile	Hyacinth
Hellebores	Crocus	Canary Ivy

MARCH
CAMELLIA
Berberis darwinii
Magnolia
Prunus spinosa (sloe)
Viburnum burkwoodii

Viola gracilis major.		Anemone blanda
Alder	Wallflower	Daffodil
Ambretia	Doronicum	Narcissus
Epimedia	Pasque flower	Arabis
	Tulips	Muscari

APRIL
ORNAMENTAL CHERRY
Mahonia aquifolium
Spurges (euphorbia)
Paeony
Clematis montana

Hyacinth	Leucojum aestivum
Chionodoxa lucillae	Tulips
Euryops pentata	

MAY
LILAC
Abutilon vitifolium
Choisya ternata
Clianthus puniceus
Honeysuckle. Banksia rose

Balsam Poplar	
Common flag	Cerastium termentosum
Aquilegia	
Anthemis cupiana	Dwarf phlox
Stock	Star of Bethlehem

JUNE
PHILADELPHUS
Clematis jackmanii
Judas Tree
Rosa Canarybird
Laburnum
Viburnum opulis sterile

Roses	Foxglove	Dwarf companula
Bearded Iris	Antirrhinum	Gladiclus
Rock roses	Oriental poppies	Nigella
Hardy geraniums	Companula persicifolia	

9

JULY
SPANISH GUM CISTUS
LANDANIFERUS.

Rhus
Buddleia
Leycesteria formosa
Clerodendron tritochomum

Phlox paniculata   Oenothera missouriensis
Penstemons   Gladiolus   Lathyrus
St Johns Wort   Crocosmia   Montbretia

AUGUST
HYDRANGEA

Fuschia
Calceolaria
Bignonia capreolata
Passion Flower.

Lilium henryi
Lavatera   Acanthus   Hemerocallis
Petunia   Tiger lily   Dahlia
Larkspur   Gladiolus   Agapanthus

SEPTEMBER
CARYOPTERIS
CLANDONENSIS

Sedum spectabile
Crab apples
Ceanothus 'Gloire de Versailles'
Michaelmas daisies

Amaryllis
Geraniums (zonal)   Japanese anemone
Sunflower   Dwarf cyclamen
Zauschenia cana   Crinum powellii alba

OCTOBER
ROWAN

Elderberry
Hebe
Chrysanthemums
Autumn crocus
Nerines

Virginia creeper   Cape gooseberry
Nerines
Pampas grass

NOVEMBER
PRUNUS SUBHIRTELLA
AUTUMNALIS

Acer purpurea
Cotoneaster horizontalis
Berberis thunbergii
Schizostylis coccinea
Spindle Tree

Ivy
Hydrangea hortensia 'Hamburg'

DECEMBER
ARBUTUS UNEDO

Holly
Elaeagnus pungens
Blue conifer
Golden conifer

Rose hips.
Viburnum laurestinus.

10

CONTENTS

JANUARY

What a joy the winter flowering jasmine is (jasmine nudiflorum) naked in its gaiety. And there beside the brave pencil spikes of the Algerian iris (Iris stylosa, now called Iris unguicularis). I preferred it being referred to as a stylus type pen. They should be picked in bud and it is my delight to watch them open during breakfast. A pendulous swing of a petal, then another and hey presto! a dainty iris smiles upon the world. They are easy to grow but hate being moved. They need a south facing sheltered spot. In the summer comb out any dead leaves with a hand fork so that the sun can bake the fleshy roots.

When the jasmine has finished flowering cut away all the brown stems. The green ones left will thrive and bring masses of flowers the next year.

It is surprising how many established flowers go on blooming in January. We have many rose buds still lingering on. These I cut for the garden's good. They don't last long indoors but the bushes must be allowed their winter sleep. I prune down to a bud which is facing outwards. The blue daisy (felicia amelloides) has survived the hard frosts last December. It is a half hardy perennial enjoying the present mild weather and showing many flowers on the rockery.

By taking cuttings in August and bringing them indoors in October we can guard against losing this happy plant.

There is a hardy pink cheerfully flowering and the heavenly blue rockery plant (lithospermum diffusum) has a few gentian blue flowers on its small evergreen leaves.   An early primrose has flowers peeping shyly low down in their leaves and the first snowdrops are out.

The pink bergenia ~ this is a giant saxifrage~ has begun its incessant display   (it's the flower at the bottom of the January garland on page 12) and the forsythia buds are a little plumper everyday.   This is when I prune off the ones which are taking too much light from the other plants and over reaching into the paths and bring them indoors. Soon the warmth brings them out and I know that Spring is on the way.

To-day a splendid bonfire.   Isn't it satisfactory when it burns without fuss? I find the way to achieve this is to put the dry wood and prunings in a heap. These I leave to dry in the wind for some weeks.   Then, when the spirit moves me, out I go with old newspapers and push these under the pile.   Usually the fire catches immediately and then from my second heap of less combustible material I feed the flames.   When there is a hole in the middle I rake the sides in and give it a good bang down. Gradually all is consumed.   Often I make a fire last several days and at the end have a heap of that beautiful bonfire ash left which, if sprinkled carefully, gives a feed to the shrubs and a snub to the weed seedlings which seem to detest it.

Our worst enemy is the butterbur or winter heliotrope. In January it smells divine, but its roots! Snap one off and redouble its life force. Beware its Latin   name: PETASITES FRAGRANS. I have seen it advertised in catalogues! Don't buy.

The blue grey leaves of the RUE are beautiful and gleam in the Winter sunshine. Rub them to release their astringent smell.

15

What a time of thrusting it is. The first sweetly scented violets (VIOLA ODORATA) are just beginning to bloom. The perfume seems to come from the leaves rather than the flowers.

The early species crocus is trying to blossom but looking a little pathetic as the birds have eaten most of its buds.

The daffodil spears are up and shooting daily. Soon the first buds will appear. The marbled leaves of the hardy cyclamen grow in charming rosettes and their corkscrew curls of seeds are seeking reinterment in the earth. Already I can see that the buds in the hyacinths are going to be pink. These hyacinths were given to me in Christmas bowls two years ago but they have naturalised in the rockery and come up every Spring. There is even a mixed up aubretia which confidently considers Spring is here. On the edge of its great cushion of leaves one or two blooms are flowering bravely.

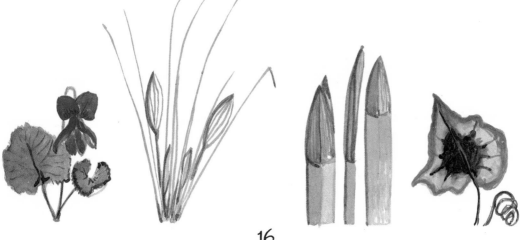

16

The pundits say that aubretia should be pruned hard back in the early Summer when they have finished flowering. I have noticed that the best aubretia in our village grow on a wall where no-one ever touches them. They get bigger and more covered in bloom each year. The foolish one that is already flowering missed being pruned last year.

When they are pruned it is a good idea to place the prunings where you would like fresh seedlings. After a few weeks they may be gathered up and shortly afterwards the little plantlets will be found. The ones left undisturbed do best but if there are too many they can be thinned out and the thinnings transplanted elsewhere.

I like aubretia best when golden alyssum is growing alongside. (Alyssum saxatile). There is nothing like bright yellow to enhance purple flowers. The two colours compliment eachother marvellously.

The garden flowers and shrubs, both the cultivated ones and those I so admire growing wild which I encourage, behave like a fashion parade. At the turn of the year

it is all evergreen and red.　Holly berries.
hips, haws and pyracanthus.　Then early
in January a delicate mauve is "in".
The lilac blue Iris and species crocus.
Sometimes a little contrasting pale
yellow comes in as if to touch the outfit with a
little brightness.　Then it all fades to a pale pinky
white.　The viburnum bodnantense scents the
air.　Viburnum laurustinus has shiny evergreen
leaves and is pink in bud - white in flower - but no
perfume.　In the rectory garden the first snowdrops
are out and the churchyard has a few daisies in flower.

　　We had an American who stayed at the hotel.
She wanted a "real English lawn" for her home in
the States.　She had scoured the Nurseries for a
grass seed mixture with "those dear little white
things in".　When we broke into helpless
laughter she looked cross.
　　"It's a conspiracy!　No one will tell
me how you do it."
Explanations about our yearly
endeavours to eradicate
the daisies were
fruitless.

　　Blackthorn or Sloe
is plumping up in
the bud on its dark

18

spikes.

What an outsize name: Bellis
perennis is for the common daisy.

The secret with snowdrops (galanthus) is to
catch them as they finish flowering and lift them
while still in strong leaf.   They can then be
divided – a few put back where they were before
and the rest planted elsewhere.   By doing this
annually sheets of these lovely flowers will
eventually come into being.

I was searching for primroses
and smelt an exquisite fragrance.
It was the spiky Berberis
type Mahonia japonica –
Well into flower so early in the
year.   I snapped a piece off –
being a long way away from my
secateurs.   I marvelled at the livid
yellow of the wood.   It flowers
each January and is well
worth a place in the shrubbery,
although its leaves are far
more unkind than holly.
I still have a sore
thumb but my sitting
room is still full of its
sweetness.

20

Mahonia japonica.

21

My vegetable garden is dug. I've put 6" from the compost heap all over it and stolen a 5cwt truck's worth of good earth from my son's fertile land. Our soil is thin, chalky and hungry. I hope John won't notice this amount out of his 6 acres!

Now for the pleasant job of choosing the seed. It is three tiny pieces 'borrowed' back from the lowest cliff. One is about 15'x4' and the other two similar in proportion. I'm going to protect the seaward edge of the highest bed with posts and heavy polythene to try to get earlier outdoor tomatoes. Last year the wind was very unkind to them.

There is room for a ten foot row of runner beans, two or three spaghetti marrows ~ my favourites. They need not be cooked whole to get their spaghetti like threads. Picked young they are equally good cut up into cubes, skin pips and all, and simmered with a chopped up onion in butter with the lid on.

I shall have the tomatoes on the southern edge and a few plants of perpetual spinach and some lettuces. Usually I find room for ½ lb of shallots so that I can harvest a ropeful for my special sauces. They must go in now. How the roots like to pull them up. Until well rooted they need a

Marjoram or Oregano   Tarragon (in bud)   Chive   Mint   Rosemary

daily inspection so as to put the pulled ones safely back.
I find the beans do so much better if planted in situ and
not too early.   Somehow I shall contrive room for a row of
Sugar peas (pois mange tout).   I like the perpetual
spinach as the stems can be lightly cooked and used as a salad
with French dressing, or they are good served hot with butter,
béchamel or cheese sauce~ two vegetables for the price of one.
My marrows grow down the cliff and ripen in the sun.
                    For the HERB GARDEN amongst the great
                    number available the eight MUSTS are:
                    Marjoram, Tarragon, Chives, Mint,
                    Rosemary, Sage, Parsley and Thyme.
                    Parsley can be sown in Spring but it is
                    important to re-sow in August because
                      this latter row will keep going all the
                      Winter.   After sowing water the row
                    with a kettle of boiling water. I think
                      this kills the carrot fly in the soil
                      and gives the seeds a chance to germinate
                    instead of being eaten. They are slow to move.

Sage

Parsley

Thyme

SEED LIST

French bean: Dobie's Violet podded stringless climber which crops a week before the runners. Very pretty and the pods turn green as they touch boiling water. I find climbers are better as the pigeons allow me a few more for my own use.

Runner bean: Sutton's Prizewinner ~ it gives a heavy crop of excellent textured medium length pods.

Peas. As a change I thought I'd try Dobie's Snap pea. "They" say the pods are meatier than my old favourite Sugar peas.

Spinach: The Perpetual or Leaf beet.

Tomato: Harbinger. 4 in my bedroom which has a glass porch French window and the rest on the cliff.

Marrow. Sutton's Vegetable spaghetti

Lettuce. Dobie's mixed varieties. This should give me lettuces all Summer & into the Autumn. I'll sow a pinch fortnightly.

Endive. (Chicorées frisées) Suttons. Well worth growing and add a bit of interest to a green salad.

If I had the room I'd grow Celeriac, Sprouting broccoli, Kohl Rabi, Beetroot, Carrots & Broad beans. I like to grow vegetables that can be gathered fresh. Bought ones are all right but never have the magic of the earthy ones grown at home.

Suttons offered me a free packet of seed so I thought I'd try Hamburg parsley which is meant to have parsnip type roots of distinctive flavour!

Now let us hope for a good harvest, sun & rain in moderation and busy bees to do their bit.

24

Prunus subhirtella Autumnalis ~ the winter
flowering cherry.

It flowers for weeks in
Winter and there should
be one in every
garden.

It takes a bit of room and grows
to the size of a standard pear
tree eventually.   When everything
is at its lowest ebb, bravely it shows
the flag and promises that the sun
will return and life Spring
once more.

The strawberry tree is flowering while still
showing its red fruits. The buds do not
appear to like them. The Portuguese,
I am told, make a liqueur from
these tasteless but
attractive fruits.
This, too, makes a large
evergreen bush.

Arbutus ~ The Strawberry Tree.
(The bell shaped flowers are waxy).

25

February

What good value the hellebores
are now.   So many varieties. The
beautiful Christmas Rose (helleborus
niger) which I cannot get to flower
by Christmas but glorious in its white
flowers now.   The little green bells
tipped with scarlet (hellebore foetidus) and
the large pale green flowered hellebore viridus
which grows about fifteen inches tall is the most
artistic of the lot.   Soon we shall have the pink
Lenten lilies (helleborus orientalis).
      Then there is helleborus corsicus with its
small prolific green flowers with golden centres and
shining spiky tough leaves. This grows tall - about 3'.
      The Christmas Rose likes a shaded spot
and is delicious to slugs.   Put grapefruit
shells around to spoil their appetites.
      Garrya elliptica grows into a handsome tall
bush. It has evergreen leaves and during late
January and early February is gaily decked with its
plenteous long catkins.   It is also called the Tassel
bush and grows happily against a north wall.
      The daffodil bud after being painted was put into
water and opened in the warmth of my sitting room. I did
not know that they would open if picked so very early.

27

The Cornelian cherry (Cornus mas) is a mass of bloom. How very yellow they are. They come before the leaves on naked stems and sprinkle their golden pollen liberally over everything. The pavement was yellow under this bush. It grows about six foot high but dislikes our chalky soil. The one illustrated was growing in Sussex ~ not Bonchurch.

The crocuses are carpeting the earth. The early warm sunshine opens them into shining stars. As long as their green growth is not disturbed they come back each year and increase and multiply.

The short little Iris reticulata is so beautiful. It lasts well indoors. The dark blue flowers fail to show up against the brown earth but brought indoors their beauty can be better appreciated. The yellow Iris danfordiae shows up better but I find it hesitant to flower.

I've just been staying in Steyning and managed to hoe all the beds in the garden there. This is the time to get the little annual

28

weeds when they first start to appear. One touch with
a Dutch hoe through their first tiny leaves takes seconds.
Left for a week or so they grow into strong plants and
carpet the soil. Then it takes days to get rid
of them.

I cut back the evergreen holm oak
because it was hiding the view of the Downs.
Cutting with a tree saw on a long pole it
is possible to thin out without hurting
the tree. The secret is to cut small
boughs flush against the bole of
the tree. Then paint the wound
over with special tree paint and no
harm is done.

I had a splendid bonfire
and burnt up about three years'
rubbish. The ash was sprinkled on
the cleaned soil.

In Sussex the hazel catkins
were ahead of the Island ones
and the tightly closed buds
of the pussy willow came out
after a day or so in a warm
room.

But the Island ground cover
was way ahead. Our yellow

29

crocuses are nearly over and now there is a delicate carpet of bluey mauve in the glade. I'm not sure of the proper name for these crocus as they were bought in a job lot.

Every year I rejoice at the forwardness of our low growing flowers. Then I go to England and find the trees have fatter buds and that the hazels, willows and witch hazels have passed ours. I can only put it down to the sea breezes.

Pussy willow cuttings are easily rooted. If these are chosen when the willows are in flower one can ensure getting the male golden catkins; the females are a demure silvery green, good for the flower arranger but nothing like so showy.

When I steal shoots from the hedgerow I always use sharp secateurs or my long-arm. It is a telescopic one and just fits into my tiny car. Then I prune as if picking from my own garden so as not to harm the wild bush. I cut hard against the main stem so as not to cripple future growth and then cut again just below a node before putting the twigs in water. I enjoy the catkins followed by the delicate green foliage. After a few weeks good water roots develop. I harden these off putting them outside daily and eventually settle them in gritty soil in the wettest part of the garden. One is growing happily behind the water butt where it gets the excess overspill of rainwater.

Often I take a tiny portion of a wild flower and naturalise it on the Rectory wall, in the churchyard or on my rockery. I know this is not encouraged but I have a fine patch of toadflax got this way. When I repassed the place that I had pilfered I found that the County Council in their wisdom had sprayed the lot with weed killer. Surely it is good to harbour our wild flowers? I took one tiny cowslip plantlet. Now I have self sown cowslips all over my cliff and this year I intend to transplant the excess into the churchyard where they will give pleasure to so many & I hope will increase & multiply.

When I got back to Bonchurch I found
the Lenten lily (hellebore orientalis)
was in full flower.

This morning I tackled the last few yards
of virgin cliff. At the top of the lowest
precipice I toppled a dead tree trunk
and was very sad when it landed on
my new Sussex trug basket.

Then with a mattock, first making
a few steps so that I could stand, I
chopped the earth and weeds away
from the rock leaving it clean.
Next down to the bottom
to sort out the spoils.
The good earth was forked
in to the narrow strip
below, convolvulus roots
put into a basket ready for the dustbin sack
and weeds were dug into the new bed. The deep
rooted docks and valerian were placed on the
bonfire with dry grass, twigs and the like.

My favourite tools are a digging fork ~ a
spade is seldom useful ~ a mattock for chopping
and digging in the loose rocks, a Dutch hoe, a
hand fork, trowel, secateurs, longarm, wire rake

tree saw, a wheelbarrow and a large sheet of strong material two yards square with four handles at the corners. The latter is ideal for carting rubbish up the steps when the barrow is useless.   I cut the lawn with a Flymo and use a Needie to trim the edges. As my lawn always finishes in rocks this spinning fishing line is the ideal tool.

It has taken me three periods of two hours to clear this last piece. The loose rocks were heaped into a dry stone wall to delineate the new bed.   This piece of cliff garden is about fifteen foot high, ten yards wide and the bottom bed about three foot wide.

I put in some root cuttings from the globe artichokes and to-morrow I shall plant the shallots ~ a bit late but in time enough I hope to harvest a good crop.

The root cuttings of the globe artichoke (Cynara) were taken in November and overwintered in a sheltered spot.   I expect farther north they would need a cold frame. Cut them off with a sharp knife as near the root as possible.   They soon make well rooted plants if put into a mixture of grit and compost.

Originally these artichokes were grown from seed. Raised in small pots on the window sill of my bedroom they were started in March and planted out in May. They made good strong plants.   The following year

33

all flower buds were cut off when the size of walnuts and
eaten whole. They cook quickly when this young and taste
good with molten butter.   By allowing the plants not to
overtax themselves really large chokes can be harvested
the following year.   The young thick stems are just as delicious
as the chokes and I cut them with about six inches attached.

       The plants are greedy feeders and should be well
mulched with well rotted manure and/or compost in the
Autumn.

                While we await the spring of the year little
          bursts of colour appear. There is a row of
                blue pansies in Harry's cottage garden.
                Great blue heads sit atop tiny stunted
                leaves.   My Corirzilla is in full
                fig.   This golden bush flowers all
                winter with its bright yellow pea
                like bunches of flowers. The
                bush is about three foot high
                and has pretty foliage in winter
                and in summer when the
                flowers are gone. The
                seed pods are not unattractive
                and little self-sown bushes
                appear ready to be
                transplanted or
                given away to friends.

Whenever there is a lull among my flowers I like to search out neighbouring gardens to see what I should be growing in order to have a continual succession of blooms.
I got as far as the Ventnor Botanical Gardens this week and found their Rosemary already in flower. I always admire their yellow daisy bush (Euryops pentata). This grows about four foot high with soft grey green feathery leaves and a mass of yellow flowers. I have grown it from cuttings but lost my three large bushes in the frosty winter two or three years ago. I have another cutting coming on well. I shall have to find it a more sheltered position. The Botanical Gardens are about a hundred foot lower down the cliffs than I. It is extraordinary what a difference this makes. Frost flows like a river and if its path of destruction is watched it is possible to find a protected spot under a rock at the foot of one of the ledges.

While I was on holiday in Genoa a few years ago I brought back a root cutting of an iris. It looks like an ordinary bearded iris until it flowers. Then it sends forth long shoots of flowers which are blue and grow in pairs right down the stem like orchids. I chose one of these sheltered spots for it and now it is a large healthy looking plant and I am hoping it will flower this year.

35

Perhaps I shall be able to draw it later on.

In the Botanical Gardens under the protection of a high west wall with a southern aspect the beautiful white camellia is in full flower. Camellias need a southern position shaded from the early morning sun. It is the early rays on frosted blossoms that causes burning and browning. This wall trained bush about fifteen foot high is shaded from the east by a stand of pines.

I don't think position is always given enough care. When I take wild flowers from hedgerows I always think about the points of the compass. There is no need to carry one about. Look for the sun, even if its not out there is always an extra brightness in the sky. By transplanting to a

similar position many disappointments can be avoided.
At noon the sun is due south, at first light east and it sets
in the west. Using a bit of calculation a near approximation
is simple to work out.

As I left the gardens I saw the alders were
in fine catkin. These trees grow in the car park
nowhere near any water, which I thought they
needed, and make attractive trees with their
catkins in spring followed by dainty cones
later. The dark brown cones of
last year are still hanging on
and make me think of a
Japanese print.

In a near garden was
a bright red bush of
cornus sibirica. This
is the Westonbirt Dogwood.
The shoots were about eight foot
high. To get these spectacular
shoots the bushes should be cut well
back in Summer so as to encourage
the vigorous highly coloured young
growth.

A good rule for pruning is to do
it as the flowers of shrubs fade.

Cut out the centre growth hard back to large stems. Then tackle the outside of the bush taking care to cut back to outwards facing buds so that the centre does not become cluttered again. Every twig longs for a place in the sun.

Near to the red stems of the dogwood was growing a heap of the attractive variegated ivy (Hedera canariensis). This gives good colour in the winter sunshine and shows up against the dark earth.

Sharing the shelter of the wall with the camellia was a fascinating shrub. I was attracted to it by the fragrance of the yellow flowers which grew in terminal clusters on the naked stems. It was marked: Edgworthia papyrifera and I see in the Hilliers Manual they say it is used by the Japanese for making high class paper and currency.

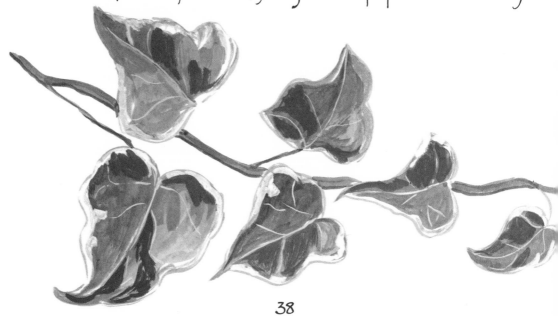

At the end of February I prune my buddleias. The common name is Butterfly bush. Every garden should have one~ if only for the pleasure of the butterflies. My varieties are Black Knight, darkest purple. the white one, Royal Red~ which I call the Bishop's Bush because it is episcopal purple. and many of the self sown wild ones which so enjoy our chalky soil. You cannot overprune a buddleia. If you cut it down to nothing still it springs again. After pruning to the desired size and shape, small side shoots taken with a heel from the discarded prunings just thrust into the earth root very easily and make strong bushes to give away for church bazaars and the like.

Then I tackle the roses.
If only the frosts would go away I would like to cut the lawn. It is looking quite shaggy.

MARCH

Sap rising in willows!
Yellow, livid green and red.
Crocus jumping out of bed.
Daffodil with tossing head!
Spring! Spring!
Winter's dead.

A splendid morning in the garden.   Just three square yards
more of the cliff to clear and I shall have finished.   I want to get
back to hoeing and tidying; to prune the roses and tie up the ramblers.
Since the frost went away it has been so wet that I have been
incarcerated.

It's raining again.   The forsythia is all but out and I
am confined indoors.   So with a jey cloth and a very weak
solution of detergent I have washed every leaf of my
pot plants.   They do so enjoy it.   Every time I tend
them I wonder why I don't do it more often.

I was pleased to see the first
Anemone blandas in flower.
There are white and blue ones too.
    The daffodils are opening fast.
By planting these in sunny south
spots through to north and darker
spots their flowering time can be
prolonged over many weeks.   I
expect you all know that you must
not pick the leaves if you hope for

41

flowers next year. The leaves have their job to do building up a healthy plump bulb full of leaves and buds for its next flowering. In the same way the leaves must be allowed to die down and not be cut off to tidy the borders. Dead heads must be removed so that the bulb makes flowers for next year instead of considering that it has justified its being by making a clutch of seeds. Cutting off their heads ~ I leave the stems so that the goodness may dry back into the bulbs ~ makes me feel a bit like Hitler.

From March onwards nearly everyday I find some new flower on the rockery. This morning I was delighted to see the dwarf Narcissus asturiensis ~ a perfect miniature daffodil together with the bright blue florets of the Chinodoxa luciliae or glory of the snow.

My cousins, who live up a mountain in Switzerland took me for a Spring walk many years ago in early May above the tree line where the snow was melting. Daily more tiny flowers appeared ~ mostly bulbous   There were crocuses and many other rock plants.

When the pundits pontificate about moving fallen leaves from rockeries I always used to think; what a pother. But having seen the rock plants in their natural home above the tree line I realised that nature and evolution have not given them a protection from heaps of leaves robbing the nitrogen from the soil. I felt a bit like Paul on the road to Damascus. It is so important whether growing indoor flowers or garden plants to consider the place they have come from. By studying their homelands and natural aspects we can get them to thrive so much better by copying their places of origin.

The dwarf yellow daisy ~ a cushion about six inches high is starting to flower: Doronicum cordatum. This is such good value and is easy to divide in early Autumn and transplant.

In my sitting room I have a large earthenware crock. It is the shape of a chinese wok and about two foot wide. In its sloping depth I grow my African violets (St. Paulia). One of them is fifteen years old. The crock is full of pebbles. The violets are in pots. I water the pebbles and not the pots. They grow strongly and flower every year for many weeks.

When I was a girl I

43

lived for some time in Mombasa.   There we grew African
violets beneath the verandah - shaded from the sun but in a good
light.   The humidity was usually between 80% and 90%.
The moist pebbles in a warm room emulate these natural
conditions with success.   I wonder if the florists fail to tell
us this because they hope to sell another plant after the death
of the former one ~~

    Closeby my Narcissus asturiensis is a little patch of an
even dwarfer one: Narcissus beryl.   What is particularly
attractive about the dwarf daffodils is that they come up
every year and increase and multiply.

                    The bright blue grape hyacinths (Muscari)
                give much pleasure but rather overdo the
                        multiplying.   Now there is
                        a large patch thriving in
                        the wasteland outside the
                        Rectory wall.
                            There are two pieces of
                        verge outside my garden and I
                            have naturalised
                            many surplus
                            plants there
                                to brighten
                                our
                                    village

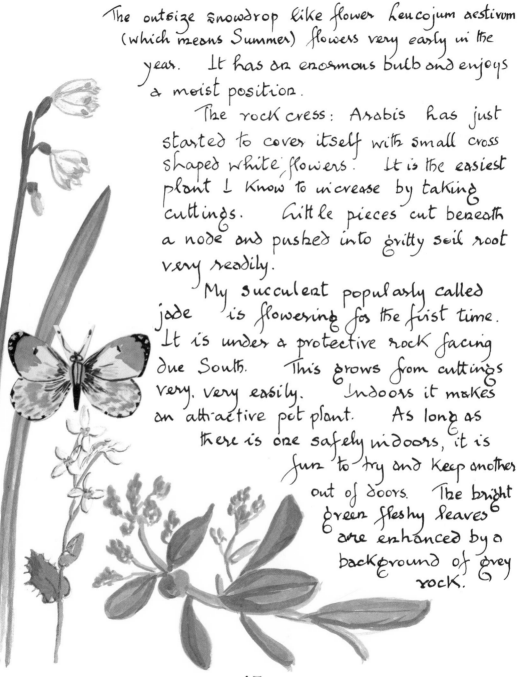

The outsize snowdrop like flower Leucojum aestivum
(which means Summer) flowers very early in the
year.   It has an enormous bulb and enjoys
a moist position.

The rock cress: Arabis has just
started to cover itself with small cross
shaped white flowers.   It is the easiest
plant I know to increase by taking
cuttings.   Little pieces cut beneath
a node and pushed into gritty soil root
very readily.

My succulent popularly called
jade   is flowering for the first time.
It is under a protective rock facing
due South.   This grows from cuttings
very, very easily.   Indoors it makes
an attractive pot plant.   As long as
there is one safely indoors, it is
fun to try and keep another
out of doors.   The bright
green fleshy leaves
are enhanced by a
background of grey
rock.

45

Blossom time is not far away.
Already the early ones are coming out.
Prunus cerasifera with its single bright
pink flowers.   Then there is what I was
taught to call Cydonia japonica.   Now
we are told to call it Chaenomeles
speciosa with its red flowers followed by
quince like fruits.
   As the years go by I enjoy the flowering shrubs
more than anything else. With a background of
blue sky, green grass and grey rocks there is
always one ready to take the floor.   They can
all be picked in bud and brought indoors
to give us pleasure a little sooner.
   Most of these blossom trees just need
a gentle prune when they have finished
flowering to keep them within bounds and a
generous bucket of compost forked in around
their roots during the Autumn.

46

Prunus triloba 'Flore Pleno' is in full
flower. Last week it was in tight bud.
I brought a spray indoors. It opened
but was many shades lighter in colour.
At last the sun is shining and
the ground relatively dry. So this morning
I managed the first cut on the shaggy
lawns with my Flymo. They look so
much better and unbelievably green
after all the rain.
Then I dug a sticky trench and
put in a thin layer of well rotted manure
and got a row of potatoes in. These were
planted for fun. They were a bag of reds,
bought at the local supermarket, which
were growing well in their polythene bags.
I cut off generous amounts with eyes and
now I wait to see if they give me a crop
of new potatoes. Last year it worked
beautifully.

It's started. The rush of Spring. The crocus are in their final colour, white with magnificent orange anthers and stamens. Curious how their colour starts a wishy-washy lavender, then vibrant yellow, deepest purple, stripey white and pure white in that order.

Some naturalised hyacinths are out. I brought one in to paint and my studio is full of its sweetness. I like them when they become nearer to their wild cousins - it is easier to see and admire their florets.

I love the early tulips. The Kaufmanianas seem to settle down and flower annually better than the larger, later ones. The red is so bright it makes me think of the guards outside Buckingham Palace.

48

First of the wild violets is out with white candytuft and self sown forget-me-nots.

My Christmas roses are doing better now that the slugs are eating the surrounding grapefruit rinds.   I have a charming viola which is suffering from slugs or snails. I cannot paint it, it is too damaged but there are many buds to come.   To-night I must go on a slug hunt with my torch.   The toads and frogs have laid copious eggs in the pond.   I go slug hunting because I will not use poison in case the song and mistle thrushes eat the tainted corpses.   So, instead I gather them all up and put them into a bucket of salted water. I hate killing anything but the nature of our rocks and their safe hiding places give these pests the upper hand. It is interesting to see the toads by torchlight winking a surprised eye at me. They all appear to have their territories and I meet them nightly in their six foot square hunting grounds.

When weeding I throw out slugs, snails and caterpillars
with cries like: "Escargots à la Bourguignonne!" The birds
don't like the green caterpillars. When I have gone in
I see from my window that they eat the green ones last.
Reminiscent of children despising cabbage.

I'm not fond of double daffodils. I find them untidy
and ill-formed. This morning they were flowering
beside a large silver leaved Cineraria maritima.
They looked at me and seemed to say: You
must know that we are beautiful. And,
of course, they come out before the
single ones. Perhaps I'm wrong.
Our tastes change as we mature.
I remember as a child disliking
geraniums. I've quite got over
that prejudice!

There is an amusing sport among the primroses.   I
think it must be a self sown hybrid with the garden polyanthus.
It looks very like our wild flower the oxlip.

   Overnight the narcissi are out.   Sheets of flowers —
creamy white petals and orange red cups together with a
delicious fragrance.   The little creamy yellow
tulip Kaufmaniana has started blooming too. Planted
about twenty years ago this little colony
continues to thrive and reappear each
year.   When the sun shines they
       open wide into
           yellow stars and
               soak up
               the welcome
               warmth.

At last the earth is dry enough to turn and I managed
to finish the rained off piece at the bottom of the lowest cliff.
Next week I'll dig a trench, put in well rotted manure,
return the earth and sow my snap-podded peas.

The aubretia are well into flower. So many attractive
shades of mauve and carmine.

The Epimedium with its clematis like flowers
is in bloom above the untidy winter leaves
with the crumpled buds of the Spring
pink leaves ready to open.

An adorable Swiss wild flower
my cousins gave me is bright carmine with
rosebud type flowers. I hope to come across
its Latin name one day.

It is almost possible to see the pulsing rush of the sap. I think of it like a blood transfusion as it springs from the roots and rushes upwards plumping buds and bursting them into flowers.

This morning my first camellia is out. I have watched its fat buds daily. Yesterday it was just that: a fat bud. To-day it is magnificent in its great pink circle of delight.

Its Latin name: Camellia japonica 'Lady Clare'.

By selecting half a dozen camellias with a knowledgeable nurseryman it is possible to have them in flower from mid-winter through to late Spring —

The same rush of sap is affecting our forest trees. I love the quotation from Cranford: "Black as ash-buds in March. ~ ~ ~ Black: they are jet-black, madam." The elm suckers are growing well. I wonder if they will manage to grow into trees once again?

The lime buds are red and the horse chestnut sticky buds the fattest of them all. The sycamore buds are a pinky green.

Birds are nesting. A song thrush disappears into a bush with a beak ful of snails. I'm delighted with the constant presence of a pair of long-tailed tits, not to mention my wood-peckers which are drum-ing away and making love volubly and noisily.

Ash   Elm

Lime   Horse chestnut

And as I watched

And as I watched the grass turned green.
The air was bright with Spring!
    The sap was pulsing into buds
    The green leaves heralding.

The sun was fading in the west,
    Flamingo pink and grey,
Enchanting as it sank to rest
    The dying glow of day.

The moon was riding on a cloud,
    Pretending it could fly.
Surrounded by a lilac shroud,
    Its beams lit up the sky.

Throw out, throw out, your drugs and pills,
    Open your purblind eyes.
Forget, forget your fears and ills.
    Let Earth be Paradise!

Sycamore

APRIL

April Fools Day and cuckoo time. In spite of sticky earth and impossible weather, to-day I planted my snap-podded peas, lettuce. moss-curled endive and perpetual spinach. It's against everything I've ever been taught but yesterday Percy Thrower was planting on Blue Peter and I felt if I waited any longer it would be next year so I'll let you know how they do. I was careful not to step on to the soil and as I couldn't rake a soft tilth I just put the seeds into the sodden sods and covered them lightly with a hand fork.

The Berberis darwinii is just coming out. It is a bush about eight foot tall and when in full flower it is dazzling in its orange dress. The first wall flowers are out. Like the crocus, the yellow ones seem to be the first. The slugs have stopped eating my viola, Viola gracilis major, since I gave them a perimiter of grapefruit rinds. This is a wonderful perennial and takes easily from cuttings. It grows in neat hassocks and makes a great show on south facing rocks. At this time of the year it has short stems. In the summer it is still flowering but has quite long stems.

The wild strawberries are in flower and a bulbous blue flower* grows in profusion outside the wall of my neighbour's house. The narcissus
* Ipheion uniflorum

57

are still doing well.   By growing
several different varieties their
flowering time can be
prolonged.

        At last the weather has changed.
Yesterday I got a third cut on the lawns
and the edges trimmed with my "needie"
To-day I got back to weeding.   Isn't
weeding therapeutic? Down on
your knees with a hand fork and
scissors and two trug baskets.
Into one go   all the annual weeds
that make such splendid compost.
Into the other go   the pernicious
weeds: dandelion, dock, sow thistle and
the like.   Also anything dry and brittle
and more suitable for the bonfire.   Then I have
a small basket for the oxalis bulbs, convolvulus
roots and similar criminals that are condemned
to the dustbin sack.   Oxalis with its tiny crescents
of reproductive growths may not even be shaken free
of soil if it is ever to be eradicated.   Its clover shaped
leaves draw our attention to its evil presence.

Brain torpid and muscles relaxed my fingers sort them out. The sun is warm on my back and I am happily philosophising about the cares of the world or thinking out my next project. At the minute the Bonchurch villagers and I are working a long tapestry for the altar kneeler and several smaller ones for the choir. We are depicting the story of the Noah's Ark.

Oxford have won the Boat Race once again.

Last week I spent a happy thirty six hours ashore in Putney with my friend and her garden was full of creamy magnolias. They love the rich silt of the Thames valley. They don't like our chalk. I have got one growing strongly in the churchyard over the wall from my garden. It is in a natural pocket of leaf mould on top of gault rocks. Even here the chalky influence sends the leaves yellow. But with the help of sequestered iron watered on according to the instructions on the packet I am hoping to succeed. I have a mimosa doing well outside my studio. This goes chlorotic and yellow every year but comes back once again after another application of sequestered iron. Apparently the chalk traps natural iron in the soil so that plants are starved of its goodness. The sequestered iron releases itself back into the earth and corrects the

59

imbalance.   I hope, once again, that it will flower
next year.   It will be seven years old then and this
does seem to be a magic number with flowering trees.

Magnolia soulangeana
    'Alexandrina'

Magnolia soulangeana
'Alba'

61

What a wonderful show
the early April tulips make.
They stand about fifteen
inches tall with enormous
heads of vibrant colour.
I like the clear colours best,
yellow, red and orange.
    A lovely extra large
flowered early is called
Apricot Beauty.   It is a

wonderful warm apricot pink.

One of the loveliest of our wild flowers is the pasque flower (Pulsatilla vulgaris). Once established it comes up year after year. It likes our chalky soil and it is possible to gather its seed and so increase its numbers. There is a posher red cultivated one but for me it lacks the charm of its grey~mauve wild cousin.

Weeding is my favourite job. I've got a pair of knee caps which men use when working on a roof. With these on it is possible to kneel down in comfort and sort out the weeds and early self-sown seedlings of garden plants. This is the time of year to deter forests of sycamore. How prolific they are ~ and yet not our most common tree. One marvels at nature's prodigality.

This is the time when the bindweed is springing. A daily visit to badly infested spots is time well spent. Pull up the shoot with a long steady pull try and get out two or three inches from beneath the soil. This really does get rid of this pest if one is persistant enough.

The yellow flowers of Mahonia aquifolium are out. They look handsome against the copper tinged evergreen leaves. I have a bush halfway up the cliff in a cleft between two enormous rocks. The golden flowers shine against the grey stone.

One of the most beautiful blossom trees in my glade

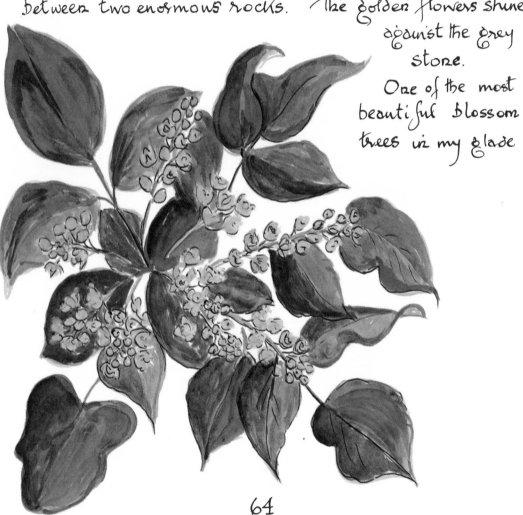

is Pyrus malus Lemoine.

The ornamental cherries are just bursting into flower. Soon the glade will be strewn with a snow of pink petals. These trees need pruning if they are in a small garden as they grow very vigorously. Tackle this job when the flowers are over and cut to keep the shape you desire. When trees have a tendency to grow asymmetrically I like to exploit this and encourage their waywardness. The Pyrus malus persists in growing in a splendid asymmetrical arc.

Another April delight is the various green yellow flowers of the spurges.

65

These grow very enthusiastically. Euphorbia epithymoides is my favourite. It grows in a neat cushion about a foot high and its flowers are more citrus yellow than green.

I have managed to naturalise a little colony of cowslips on top of one of my many clifftops. They are growing very happily and have sown themselves all over the top of the Knoll where they bask in the sun amongst chalky earth. If they were rare and came from the Himalayas – or even further afield – there would be an expensive bought plant lovingly cherished in every rock garden! They smell lovely, look lovely and thrive. More and more I am including our beautiful wild flowers in the garden.

I was having terrible trouble with a mole which was wrecking my lawn. There is an old wive's tale that the caper spurge, Euphorbia lathyrus, another of our native plants, will get rid of moles. It is quite a handsome plant ~ I use it in flower arrangements ~ and grows about three foot high. Anyway I planted one and the mole has moved on. Was it a co-incidence?

The vegetable garden is going well. The snap-podded peas put into the unfriendly drenched unprepared soil have germinated well. The potatoes and shallots are coming on. My first thinly sown pinch of mixed lettuce seed is through. Yesterday I put the new earth on top of the compost covered cliff ready for the runner beans and tomatoes. I would never have believed that the peas would have come through so well and so evenly.

Caper Spurge

Clematis montana, tightly in bud yesterday, is a riot to-day, my favourite climber. They need no pruning except for tidying them which should be seen to after they have finished flowering. The large flowered clematis should be pruned hard in February ~ although my Clematis Jackmanii (p. 107) is allowed to riot like the montanas and makes a stunning purple arch in partnership with a hardy fuschia. This grows horizontally out of the cliff and its asymmetry exploited.

To-day friends called for coffee so the weeding was abandoned. So this afternoon I justified my conscience by sowing Tomato "Harbinger" and the spaghetti marrows in pots. These are in my bedroom in the French window alcove. I used equal parts of good garden soil, council grit and well rotted compost.

I enjoy salvaging council grit. "They" sprinkle it on our steep shute during frosty weather and then sweep it up again Car wheels drive it into the curb. It is easy to glean a barrowful or two and keep it in a neat heap behind the tool shed,

At last the weather seems to have settled: back to my favourite garden technique: the Forth bridge. A quiet progress eliminating, transplanting, encouraging and admiring, two trug baskets~one full of Radio IV and tools, the other a depository for the unloved~ leap frogging over eachother in the sunshine. Blackbirds, so tame, were foraging and helping ~ beaks full. I've found one nest full of eggs~ so I must have another one.

On the eve of May the first of the fat buds on my gorgeous single paeony has burst. The plant was a present from a botanist and its Latin name is;
Paeonia Mlokosewitschii.
(Seed collected in the Caucasus c 1964.)

69

MAY

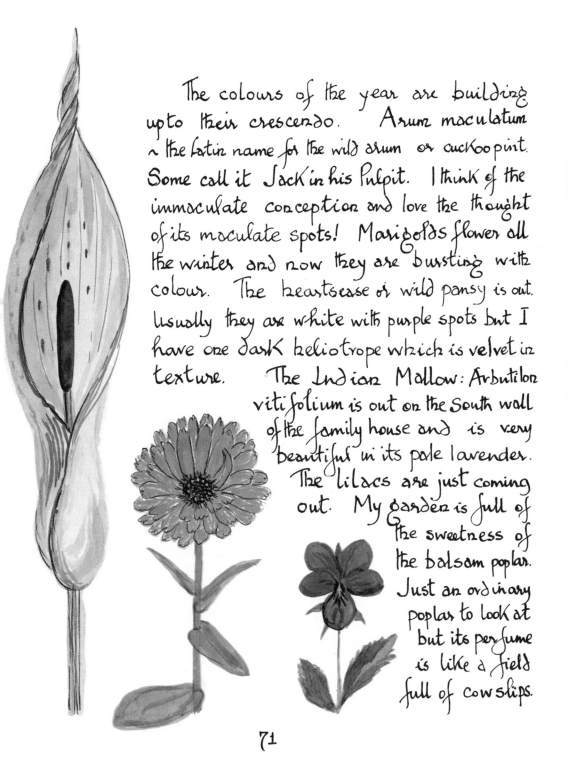

The colours of the year are building up to their crescendo. Arum maculatum ˄ the latin name for the wild arum or cuckoo pint. Some call it Jack in his Pulpit. I think of the immaculate conception and love the thought of its maculate spots! Marigolds flower all the winter and now they are bursting with colour. The heartsease or wild pansy is out. Usually they are white with purple spots but I have one dark heliotrope which is velvet in texture. The Indian Mallow: Arbutilon vitifolium is out on the South wall of the family house and is very beautiful in its pale lavender. The lilacs are just coming out. My garden is full of the sweetness of the balsam poplar. Just an ordinary poplar to look at but its perfume is like a field full of cowslips.

71

White flowers are uplifting. They glow against the green leaves. Best of all for flower arrangements. Perhaps their charm is in the shades of grey and green they harbour in the shadows of their petals. The Mexican Orange blossom (Choisya ternata) makes a rotund shrub up to five foot high. It smells delightful and has shiny evergreen soft leaves like little hands.

On the rocks the daisy flower Anthemis makes great cushions of grey leaves and blooms for months. If you push a slip into the earth it takes readily at almost any time of the year. After they have flowered the more unkindly you cut them back the better they do. A bit invasive but fun.

Anthemis
cupariana

72

The white candle flowers of the horse chestnut are in full fig. A favourite uncle used to wear the top of one in his buttonhole when in the City. Friends thought that it was an orchid.

Lilac time is here. Such wonderful colours are available now but still I prefer the white and natural lilacs. They last well in water if all the leaves are removed. Pick another leafy twig without flowers and they will look charming and last for days. They scent the air and with my balsam poplar the garden smells of early summer.

73

When we came to this cliff garden about fourteen years ago
there was a heap of grass like foliage which
looked as if it came from bulbs. In
a new garden one always has to wait
a twelvemonth to see what is there.
This heap of "grass" was disappointing
and nothing happened. So with
trepidation it was dug up. Thousands
and thousands of bulbs. So they were
separated and replanted here and
there. Now they are a mass of
Stars of Bethlehem and a delight.
There is a self sown Stock in a
cleft in the cliff, two foot tall
and a blaze of white petals.
The perfume is overwhelming.
Next to it on a tiny pocket in
a rock is a pinnacle
of 'Snow in Summer' —
(Cerastium tomentosum)
Lovely confined but a
disaster if it is allowed
to ramp, invade and
overcome more
delicate subjects.

This page looks quite
patriotic.   The red lobster
claw (Clianthus puniceus) a
New Zealand flower grows well
on a sheltered southern wall.
Its pealike flowers really   do
look lobsterish and are followed by peapods full of seed.
   The incredibly blue flower Alkanet,
one of our native plants is profuse.
They are used to make dye. Oddly
the roots turn cloth red.
      My snap-podded peas are
growing well but a lot are missing.
  I think they were eaten by mice. A friend
tells me, too late, that the trick is to put holly leaves
in the drill with the seed, and that mice hate having
their noses scratched.   I'll try again next year.

The beautiful red honeysuckle (Lonicera americana) is out in full splendour on a neighbour's house facing the sun on a south west wall. It smells more beautiful in the evening working to attract moths for its pollination and to ensure its success in procreation. I'm going to see if I can layer a piece so that I, too, can have its beauty in my garden.

This morning the Forth bridge technique had reached my vegetable ledges. Slugs have eaten nearly all the lettuce. They've left a few baby cos and I shall cut up grapefruit shells and scatter them round the sugarpeas and lettuce and to-night with murder in my heart I shall go out into the moonlight with torch and bucket. How I hate killing them, but it has to be done.

There were dozens of tiny black slugs in the grapefruit shells and I think I shall have to resort to poisoning them. Using a newly cleared piece of wilderness does mean that one is vulnerable to the inroads of hungry hoards.

Mid-May and this morning I planted runner beans and French beans and sowed again mixed lettuce, well flanked with strips of grapefruit shells. This purple flag was in a neighbour's garden - a great clump. When I noticed that this was a blank week in the garden I went round looking for flowers that were flourishing elsewhere. The village was aflame with common flags

77

purple and lavender.   So my mother gave me her
copy of Wallace and Barr's catalogue.   I splashed
out on buying glorious colours with enchanting names
such as Cinnamon Toast.   They have developed
well and they thrive but they do not deign to flower
until two or three weeks after their ordinary cousins
I suppose the moral is to grow both kinds ~~

   With our chalky soil acid lovers such as azaleas
and rhododendrons are forbidden fruit. So having
two conveniently placed rocks about 4' x 2' x 5'
in size with a 2'6" chasm between. I filled the open
ends with rocks and made compost for two or three
years.   Then I put a whole bale of peat on top

78

and forked it in well.   Then six dwarf azaleas were planted and this year they are a sheet of colour.   They are Scarlet O'Hara and a great treat in a chalk garden.

The Judas Tree. (Cercis siliquastrum) is opening. Little pink pea flowers straight out of the bark before the leaves. Quite easy to grow. A pot grown bush put into good tree compost, which can be bought at any garden centre, sited in a warm corner of the garden will grow away well and make a beautiful slow growing tree.

On the rockery cushions of dwarf phlox are displaying. Pale blue, pink and carmine.   The one illustrated is Phlox amoena. They are easy to grow and keep the colour going in the rockery as the aubretias start to fade.   They make rooted plantlets on their outer edges

79

which can be transplanted.

Rosa Canary Bird, a beautiful yellow single rose comes out earlier than the hybrid teas and floribundas. It grows into an attractive free standing shrub and is a mass of golden sprays from late May right through to June. It needs very little pruning; just a tidy up after it has flowered and a good mulch of manure or compost to help it make its flower buds for the following year. Almost earlier is the lovely shrub come climber, the thornless Banksia Rose. When I was a small girl Sunday in Summer dictated the wearing of a straw hat or bonnet trimmed with these yellow rosebuds and forget-me-nots!

Laburnums gave a shout of colour at the beginning of the month. They are easy to grow and ask for scarcely any maintenance.

This morning I was rained off but I managed to plant out two climbers to help hide a hideous fence my neighbours insisted on erecting, first destroying a charming Lonicera nitida hedge about eight foot tall. I put in Solanum jasminoides which grows very fast and is smothered in white jasmine like flowers. I chose it because it is flourishing in a neighbour's garden and the position is similar. The other climber is Clematis tangutica. This has yellow bell flowers and I like white and yellow together. Then I put in some petunias which have been hardened off.

June is just round the
corner and still the weather
refuses to settle.   Aquilegias
are worth growing. Once
established they come up
year after year and they are
available in a very full range
of colours.
          The Snowball Tree:
Viburnum opulis sterile is beginning to
bloom. It starts pale green and matures
into a white ball.   Both the long spurred
                aquilegias and all the Viburnums
                like our chalky soil.   The
                wild guelder rose: Viburnum
                opulis is not sterile and
                its flat heads are followed
                by showy berries in the
                Autumn.
                   The most riotous
                flowers at the
                moment are a
          bed of parrot and
     bizarre tulips.   Their zany
shapes and vibrant colours are

most eye catching and unlike the
Darwin tulips which tend to fade
away, the parrots appear to increase and
multiply.

This is a between time in the garden. The
early Spring flush is over and the bearded
iris and roses are all burgeoning but
not yet blooming.   The birds are singing
all day as if to promise us that "Sumer
is icumen in"   if only we will be patient
for a few more hours, or days ~ ~ ~

83

JUNE

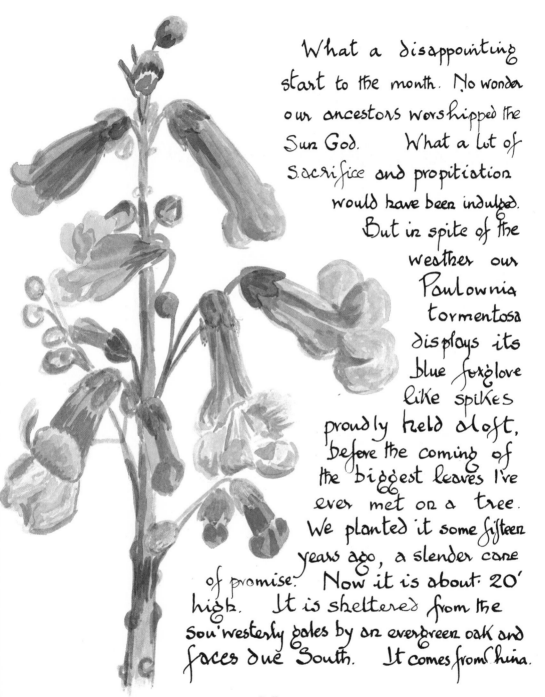

What a disappointing start to the month. No wonder our ancestors worshipped the Sun God. What a lot of sacrifice and propitiation would have been indulged. But in spite of the weather our Paulownia tormentosa displays its blue foxglove like spikes proudly held aloft, before the coming of the biggest leaves I've ever met on a tree. We planted it some fifteen years ago, a slender cane of promise. Now it is about 20' high. It is sheltered from the sou'westerly gales by an evergreen oak and faces due South. It comes from China.

85

My beautiful bearded Iris I
bought from Wallace & Barr
are now at their best.   So
many glorious colours; ~
the bright yellow of lime-
light ~ delicate blue of
Symphony and many deep
browns, golds and pure
white ones. Every year they
increase.   As they become
overcrowded I have
moved some outside pieces
to the Rectory garden. These
are now doing better than
mine and I feel the moral
of this story is to transplant
some of my own, taking
from the outer edge, replant
very high in the soil having
first forked in bone meal and

some fertiliser.   This job is best done in the Summer – July.
At last the sun is shining and encouraging
the faces of my rock roses to smile.
I've put them into the June garland – red
orange, yellow and lemon. Cuttings
taken now through to August root readily.
I just push two or three slips into the
rocky pockets and many survive. They
are technically Helianthemum and most
alpine catalogues have plenty to choose
from. The hardy geraniums are
vivid in their blue cushions
nearly two foot high and
their lower kin deck the
rocks with their pink
flowers.
    Carpets of blue
campanulas are
covering the stone in
different shades
of blue. The one on the June
garland is: C. garganica.

There are so many blooms to paint now that it is difficult to know which to choose and which to leave out, and then I feel unkind - as if the unpainted is the child not chosen for the team. Foxgloves are doing very well and I love the cream ones with their heliotrope spots. Love-in-a-Mist (Nigella) is in full flower. They dry well and keep their clear blue petals even in death. Philadelphus, the Mock Orange blossom ~ often wrongly called Syringa (which, of course, is lilac) ~ is a yearly delight with its white wax petals and delicious smell. The double is very showy. But usually I prefer the simplicity and clean shape of single blooms of almost any variety of flower.

The snapdragons or antirrhinums come up yearly. There is no need to treat them as annuals. After they have finished flowering, if they are cut back neatly they will make fresh growth and flower very early next year or give up the ghost.   I always think: "either will do." !

Philadelphus should be pruned in July and August after it has finished flowering.   It does grow very freely. If it has got out of shape it is quite in order to cut out one of the largest boughs at the root.   This can be done yearly and the bush brought gradually back to a manageable size. Destroying one main stem a year will still leave plenty of flowers. The green growth so made will flower in its second year.   This technique is very effective with most neglected shrubs and will restore most of them to health and rejuvenation.

Great oversized blooms
of mid June.   Enormous
oriental poppies; pink
red and pure white
with great   black
velvet centres.
Next to them the
beautiful   bearded
Iris~ the clear blue
of Symphony and the
tantalising golden brown
tinged with wine pink of
Cinnamon Toast.
The flowers go on and on flowering
everyday. One dies and another
opens and they flower for a full
four weeks. There are many other
colours,   purple, pure gold
dull reds with light brown
frilly translucent petals.   They
give and give and only ask for the sun
to bake their roots so that they can
make their flowers for next year.

90

91

A page in praise of the
beauty of single roses.
First of all our native
dog rose that leaps
out of a bush and
silhouettes itself against a clear sky.
Then there are the ones I bought from Hilliers of
Winchester. They subscribed so generously to our Botanic
Gardens at Ventnor that I have purchased from them
ever since. Pure white Rosa paulii, scented and rampant
on my rocks. Soft pink Rosa polliniana

which grows up from the bottom of the cliff in a less agressive manner. The delight of a dead tree festooned in veils of Wedding Day~ butter yellow in bud, white in maturity and dusky pink as it fades away.   I found the Austrian briar at Wisley thirty years ago.

It is a bright copper red and later has long elegant hips. All these roses like a well drained soil. They need only a little tidying after they have flowered and if long shoots are pegged down they become a deluge of flowers the next year.

They love my sunny rocks and their scent on the air wafts up the cliff and into my bedroom. You all have your favourite roses but don't you agree that the singles deserve a place?

93

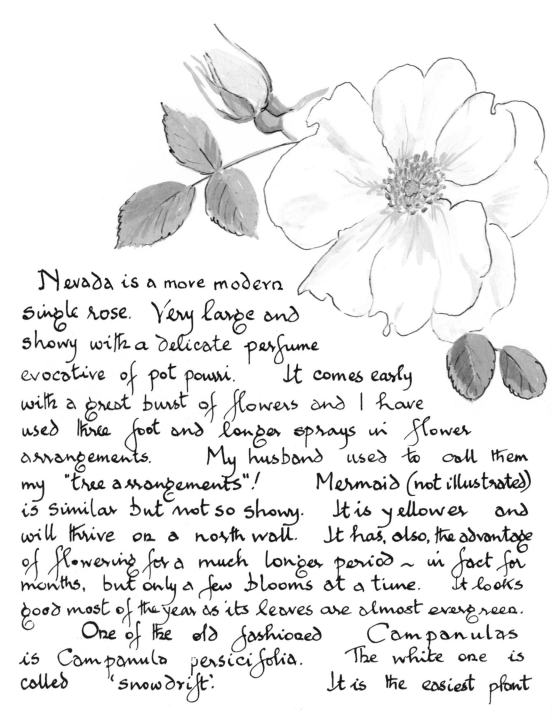

Nevada is a more modern
single rose. Very large and
showy with a delicate perfume
evocative of pot pourri.   It comes early
with a great burst of flowers and I have
used three foot and longer sprays in flower
arrangements.   My husband used to call them
my "tree arrangements"!   Mermaid (not illustrated)
is similar but not so showy.   It is yellower   and
will thrive on a north wall.   It has, also, the advantage
of flowering for a much longer period ~ in fact for
months, but only a few blooms at a time.   It looks
good most of the year as its leaves are almost evergreen.
          One of the old fashioned   Campanulas
is Campanula persicifolia.   The white one is
called   'snowdrift'.   It is the easiest plant

I know to propagate.
Just divide the clumps in
Spring. Dig up and using
two digging forks back to
back prise the roots apart
into about ten or more
divisions. Replant
and there you are! You
have a lot of plants.
The blue variety
illustrated overleaf is called:
'Telham Beauty'.
This week I used the white
ones with enormous sprays of
philadelphus (p. 89) to decorate
our church. The result was
spectacular* and they have lasted
a full week. With the seasonal
green altar cloth they looked as
if the garden had come indoors
~ which is my idea of a
successful arrangement. For me
florists flowers are almost artificial~

As the choir
all had hay-fever
was asked not to
do it again!

95

Basal cuttings of these companulas can
be taken either in Spring or Autumn. They
take best in gritty, sandy compost and
will thrive alike in sun or partial shade.

Iris foetida is one of our native
wild flowers. I am very fond of it because
it is undemanding and grows
very tidily.   However, its flowers
are almost camonflaged
in their unshowiness.

Come the Autumn this
changes and they are
very dramatic with
their bright orange
seeds which stay on
for months and if
dried carefully will
make a Winter
arrangement of
dried leaves and
grasses.   (See p. 147).

The name comes
from the odd meaty

96

smell which is in the sap. Rub a
leaf and you are in an old fashioned
butcher's shop.

Another companula which
makes a good splash of colour
at this time of the year
is Campanula glomerata
'Superba'.   It grows about
a foot high and spreads
vigourously.   Locally it's called
the twelve apostles because
its meant to have twelve florets
to a head — but mine have many more!
It, too, lasts well in water.

At last the sun is beginning
to shine and I am hoping that
the year will start to catch up
with the lateness of its seasons.
It's almost as if, having decided
to write A Gardener's Year, that the
plants and weather are just doing it
to annoy 'because they know it teases'~~

97

JULY

Half way through the year and the garden seems to be
using. The first flush of June tea roses is on the wane
and now is the time to cut back dead flowers and take
out diseased foliage. My roses are enjoying a feed of
artificial fertiliser lightly forked in. Be careful
not to go too deep and disturb the roots. Living in
such a clean air area we have terrible trouble with
black spot. Nimrod, the commercial spray is very effective
against this disease. Even so I like to pick off the
affected leaves and either burn them or wrap them up and
consign them to the dustbin. Care should be taken to collect
fallen leaves as the fungus is soil born. A good watering
with Jeyes fluid in January helps to keep the blackspot
at bay. Also I like to pick long spikes of roses.
These are beautiful in flower arrangements and give
the shrubs a chance to rejuvenate ready for their next
full flush of flowering. The rocks of the precipices
of Bonchurch are gilded with the flowers of the hardy
shrub Senecio greyi. I like the grey leaves which
are bright silver on the back. Used back to front they
make a delightful background for pink flower
arrangements. This is the time of the everlasting

99

pea: Lathyrus grandiflorus and latifolius ~ the
former about five foot and the latter ten.   They
grow forcefully and their foliage is attractive.   The
carmine flowers are prolific and from very bright pink
they fade to a curious blue shade.   The green
shoots make a good background in flower arrangement
for the sweet peas which have little spare foliage.
  We have also been successful with a white variety grown
from seed. Also a pale pink which I find wishy-washy. Former
white flowers are always the most beautiful.
        On the rock garden two dwarf varieties of
St. John's wort are making a good show. The golden
one is Hypericum polyphyllum and grows about 9"
high. There is the pale lemon variety 'citrinum'. They grow
in neat round cushions and are not invasive like the
Rose of Sharon. (p.105).   The dwarf ones are illustrated
in the July garland.   The deep gold one has a larger
flower.
        I am smugly full of virtue because this morning I
sifted compost into my wheel barrow~ Added wood ash,
bonemeal and 'growmore' and trundled two loads to
the top Iris bed.   I lifted all the bearded iris, forked the
soil, weeded and added the new earth. Then I replanted
separate rhizomes having trimmed their leaves down
to about eight inches.   Too lazy to get the hose out

100

was pleased to find that it had rained
all night. Now the sun is shining
and I hope they will flower for me
next year. I expect I'll have to
wait for two years for a real display.
'Tis ever thus. Gardening calls for
patience!

Hydrangeas do very
well in our chalky soil
but are bright pink. One
year I moved some up to
the wood into natural
leafmould which had been there
for generations. The flowers turned
blue the following year. I had
not realised the leafmould was so
acid. 2 oz of commercial alum
to 2 gallons of rainwater used
regularly will turn them an artistic
mauvy blue. If mixed with tapwater the
alum will change the flowers a curious green.
Small shoots of hydrangea pulled off with a heel
will root readily this month and in August.
    My best bush was devastated by a rock fall some
years ago. I pruned it down, sorrowfully, to ground
level. Now it is magnificent. So learning from

this accident I cut out two strong stems to ground level each autumn and consequently the bushes are getting stronger and more floriferous each year. When planting new bushes the trick is to plant them into a saucer shaped depression in the bed. Their name means 'water' and they need to collect all the rain that is going. They hate being planted on a little hillock. _

The Spanish Gum Cistus (C. londoniferus) is a very happy shrub. It grows in a neat sphere and is smothered in flowers for a good six weeks. Again it is easy to raise from cuttings taken now until late August. Its poppy like blooms unfold the purest white with attractive dark blotches and golden centres.

The vegetable garden is doing well. Although the slugs and snails had so many of my pea seedlings I am delighted with the ones they have left for me. The pea pods are fleshy and cook with the texture of a French bean and taste deliciously of green peas. The spinach is cropping well. I've had a continuous supply of lettuces from my pinches of mixed seed sown fortnightly. The only plants that have suffered with the unseasonal weather are the tomatoes and marrows. But, at last, they are moving and I'm hoping for a late crop. The target is either a very early crop or a late one. The middle time is when the professional produce is in full spate and the prices come tumbling down. The runner beans and climbing french beans are well up their poles and I'm digging good potatoes. The seeds sown are on page 24.

104

Two weeds or flowers with which I have a love/hate relationship are convolvulus and St.John's wort. I'm a firm subscriber to the definition that a weed is a plant growing in the wrong place. I declared war on the convolvulus - or bell bine - or the Elizabethan name: "Devil's guts" - perhaps the most apt - when I decided to tackle the steepest part of the cliff. I've shifted wheelbarrows full of its spaghetti like roots and pulled out all the tender shoots left each spring. When one gets away and succeeds in climbing to the top and flowers so beautifully I can only stand and admire the white trumpets. St.John's wort is equally attractive in flower and really quells other weeds but it is so invasive that it is necessary to start another war to repulse its agression. Isn't it amazing how weeds flourish in a cultivated garden? Have you ever seen a fine stand of convolvulus in a hedgerow? - unless there is a garden near.

It is as if it enjoys being chopped and pulled and decimated
Leave it alone and it chokes itself. I am told the way to get
rid of it is to dip its growing ends in a weak solution of weed
killer in the Spring. I keep on meaning to try but continue
to get a thrill from the beauty of its wayward blooms.

After the Spring burst of colour on the rockeries
when the various shades of aubretia and the gold of the
alyssum make such a show there is a pause. One of
the flowers that brighten the rocks in late July through
to September is the dwarf form of the evening primrose:
OENOTHERA MISSOURIENSIS. It has a generous number
of large funnel shaped flowers everyday
and grows between six and
nine inches high. The red
vigourous stems which carry
the growth are in themselves
attractive. It is a hardy
plant coming up yearly
increasing the area
of its spread.

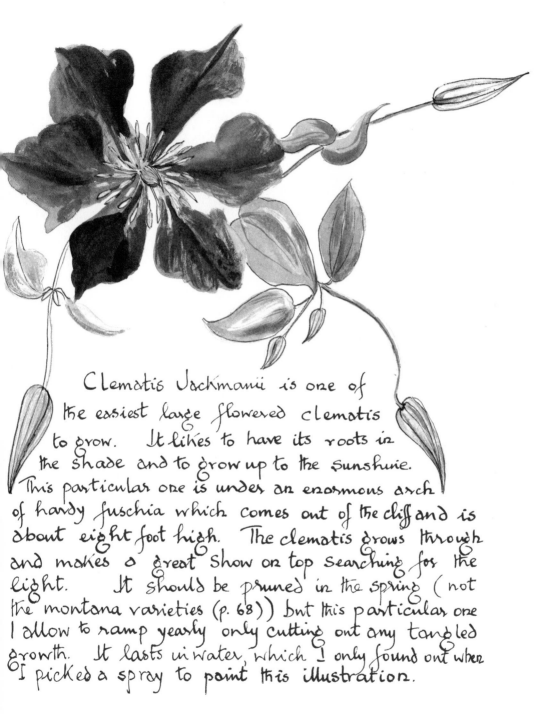

Clematis Jackmanii is one of
the easiest large flowered clematis
to grow.   It likes to have its roots in
the shade and to grow up to the sunshine.
This particular one is under an enormous arch
of hardy fuschia which comes out of the cliff and is
about eight foot high.   The clematis grows through
and makes a great show on top searching for the
light.   It should be pruned in the spring (not
the montana varieties (p. 68)) but this particular one
I allow to ramp yearly only cutting out any tangled
growth.   It lasts in water, which I only found out when
I picked a spray to paint this illustration.

Gladiolus make a great show. The earliest is Gladiolus byzantinus which grows almost wild on our cliffs. It is illustrated on p. 87. The next to bloom is Gladiolus nanus. This dwarf is in many beautiful colours and grows in dainty sprays. There is one in the July garland and the red one on this page. Usually I buy these either from Bloms of Leawesden. Watford or Van Tubergen of 304a Upper Richmond Road West, London, S.W. 14. I find that the mixed Gladiolus nanus offered include many attractive shades and cost less to buy than the named varieties. Next come the butterfly and primulinus types. They grow between 2½' and 3' and need no staking. Finally the stately giants up to 5' high. When

Two common Sedums

Viola gracilis major

we lived in Twickenham about thirty years ago I was given a useful tip by an elderly professional gardener. Dig a hole 9" deep and put in a handful of poultry manure, then a handful of sharp sand, next the corm, then another handful of sand, and finally the earth. The result is flamboyant and I always try to plant the large flowered varieties this way.

The Viola gracilis major is just about over and I have given it a 'hair cut' and taken many cuttings. I find these root best in a shady place. Then I move them when they start to grow away and need a sunny position in which to develop.

The leaves of the Rhus glow in the Summer sunshine. This is a slow growing shrub and gives colour most of the year. It looks particularly good grown near a golden leaved shrub such as a free standing golden yew.

Buddleia love our chalky soil
and the butterflies love the Buddleia.
This one, my favourite, is called
"Royal Red" but I call it the Bishop's
bush because it is exactly the
episcopal purple of a bishop's shirt.
All the buddleias are attractive and
very easy to propagate.   They should
be pruned hard back in February
Little side shoots pulled off from the
prunings with a heel just pushed
into the soil root readily.   There
is a beautiful white one, an almost
navy blue/purple called "Black Knight"
and many mauve/blues from the original
wild ones which came from China.
    They brighten the latter half of
July when flowers are scarce.
Phlox paniculata is a useful
perennial border plant which
flourishes once established. They
are available in many shades
and make flower spikes about
three foot high (Not illustrated)

A Himalayan shrub that grows wild in Bonchurch is Leycesteria formosa. It grows about six foot tall and has pleasant white flowers which droop in clusters much embellished by the red, purple bracts. Later it has purple fruits which the birds squabble over.

It is a good background maker in flower arrangements and lasts well in water.

It should be pruned hard in April to encourage the growth of strong young shoots. The birds distribute it widely and it pops up everywhere — even from crevices in the rocks of the cliff.

Penstemons, Crocosmia, and Montbretia are all in flower but I will show them next month — also the bright yellow flowers of the calceolarias.

AUGUST

For me August is a month of
luscious flowers which
grow from fleshy roots, corms
and bulbs.   All the lilies
are coming into flower.
The old fashioned
Montbretia, useful as a
background flower in
arrangements, is far outshone
by the much showier Crocosmia
with its flowers thrusting forward
in a dazzling orange.   The
tiger lilies are out and vibrant in
their flame colours.
Montbretia is apt to grow into too
dense a clump. Every two or three years
dig them up when they are dormant and
you will find "necklaces" of their corms.
Snap these apart and choose the best ones.
Then replant them; having added some
compost or manure to the soil; about four
inches deep and four inches apart. This
way you get far more and far better blooms.

The Gladiolus nanus are over and gone followed
now by the primulinus type with stems near
three foot high ~ the flowers spaced so that w
can enjoy the beauty of their individual
florets. This picture shows the top of the
spike. There were five more florets which
would not fit on to the page.

The old fashioned Day Lily (Hemerocallis)
gets its name from the daily appearance o
another luscious flower. They grow into
great clumps about two foot wide and three
foot tall and need very little attention. The
colour ranges from yellow to a rusty red. My
favourite is the middle orange shade

The Penstemons are doing well. I first saw them at Wisley and bought seed. Every year since they have flowered well in mixed colours of pink, scarlet, salmon and claret.

The dahlia, too, was raised from a packet of seed. The mixture gave me a splendid selection of colours from citrus

yellow, through auburns and reds to purple. Many perennials are easy to grow from seed. These two varieties were scattered in a shady seed bed and then transplanted.

115

The present joy is a large clump of
Agapanthus. There are thirteen spikes
standing about three foot high.
Behind them are two spikes
of the tall five foot lily:
Lilium Henryi. Each
spike has more than
twenty florets and they
are bowed down into the

Lilium
henryi

Agapanthus

ue heads of the Agapanthus. This clump is very large
nd the roots so near to the surface that it is difficult to keep
free from weeds. I top dress the surface soil both in the
utumn and in the spring with a rich mixture of leaf mould,
eat and rotted manure first teasing out the weeds. Always
damage a few roots but the lilies do not seem to be
armed. The flowers are at their best for more than
ix weeks. One year I made the mistake of letting
e seed set. The result was lots of plantlets which I
aised on the window sill beside the French windows. But
ie next year the Agapanthus failed to flower. So now
cut off the flowers as they fade. Just the very tops,
e fleshy stems are allowed to die right back feeding
ie roots for next year's flowering. The bonus
rom this sad tale is a hedge of Agapanthus in the
arden of the family hotel. The plantlets took
ree years to come to their flowering.
    Lilies are not fond of our chalky soil.
Henryi seems to be the exception. For three years
t carried one great spike with a great thick stem.
This year it carries two spikes and the Tiger lily
is thriving also.
    The fuschias are in the same bed. They seem
o flower from December to December with a slight
ause in the spring. Now they are at their very best.

117

My favourite is "Mrs Popple"
with its purple flowers with red
calices. The leaves **are** a pretty
golden green and they grow in a
thick bush which cascades over
the rocks. A winter or so ago
I thought I had lost them. They died
right back to the earth. I pruned all
the dead twigs and hoped. From the
base fat red healthy buds started to develop and
they seemed to grow as fast as the beanstalk in
the pantomime. In a way the severe set back
of that particular winter seems to have benefitted
the shrubs. Now they are a better shape, bushier
and more floriferous.

Down here in our Island we have hedges of the very
hardy fuchsia: magellanica which has much
smaller and daintier flowers. When a child my
daughter called these: "Dancing ladies" which
describes them so well.

Cascade is a lovely type which naturally
grows downwards. It makes falls of colour down

the rocks.   They all grow towards the sun and always face the south. They will not fall down a north rock. There are many different names in this class and a good choice of colour.   All fuchsias root readily from cuttings taken now. Little flower-less side shoots pulled off with a heel and planted into good gritty soil and then covered with a sheet of glass and shaded soon make side shoots and rootlets. Don't worry if the leaves fall off.   New buds will soon appear.   When they have rooted pot them up singly or plant them where you want them to flower.

August is the time to plant parsley if you like to pick it throughout the winter. So I planted mine this morning and then poured a kettle of boiling water right down the row.   Also some more of my mixed lettuce seed.   These continue to give me a succession of different types of lettuces.

I expect you have noticed that I do not try
to grow many annuals.   Basically I
consider the necessity to resort to
annuals as a confession
of failure.   In a well
planted garden there
should always be some
perennial or a shrub
or blossom tree in peak
condition through each
week of the year.   This cuts
down the initial planting to just
over fifty species and there is
a suggested list on page 8.
However there are a few types of
annual that help us to colour
at lean times of the year. Lavatera
or Mallow is one of these. Most of them
are bright pink and grow easily from
thinly scattered seed into bushy plants
about three foot high with a good show
of trumpets. They like sun. For a shady
position I find Petunia very useful.   They

are best raised from seed started indoors.

Another excellent annual, particularly for use as a cut flower is Larkspur ~ one of the delphiniums.   They come in a wonderful range of colours: pinks, blues, white, lavender and many shades between.

The seed should be scattered where it is intended to flower. If they are transplanted they grow very small. So sow thinly and thin out to get good healthy plants.   They dry well and keep their colours if hung upside down in a draughty shady place~ picked when just starting to open and look lovely with autumn grasses.

The Passion Flower appears to be late this year. Usually it comes into bloom in July. The flowers are handsome. This variety: Passiflora caerulea, has green white petals and sky blue filaments. The five yellow anthers, some say, depict the five wounds in Christ's body, the three parts of the stigma represent the Holy Trinity and the ten petals the ten faithful Apostles. Later orange fruits develop. These are edible but tasteless. The Grenadilla has purple fruits and, although very similar, is far more tender and will not live outdoors. Plant caerulea on a South wall and be patient. When it is three years old, usually, it goes berserk and clings anywhere flowering generously. It is easy to grow from seed or a warm window sill. The latin name of Grenadilla is: Passiflora edulis.

For me Acanthus is an architectural plant. It is large and spiky and swirls in bends of movement. No wonder the Heralds have chosen it for exploitation in adorning their coats of arms, helmets and escutcheons.

The flowers stand up majestically in the wonderfully formed leaves and have an almost artificial perfection of form. Once established they appear yearly. They like a sunny south position on a well drained site. This plant was raised from seed brought to me from Italy. It is always grown in reconstructed historic Roman gardens as a typical plant.

123

Bignonia capreolata   is an evergreen climber
which has mounted to the   top of the front of the house.
It must be quite thirty foot high and is covered with
orange/red trumpets.   Certainly it is on the south face
of the house with an eight foot west wall to protect its roots,
but I think it is much hardier than usually considered.
It came through the terrible blizzard of 1962/63 when
we were snowed in and imprisoned in the village for weeks.
The whole place was frozen up and water was being
delivered daily in milk churns by the Council.

The Glory Tree is coming into its
prime. Its Latin name: Clerodendron
trichotomum. The bracts are a
deep crimson and the flowers a
starry white. Later it has blue
berries. It likes to be planted
in full sun on a well drained
slope. After dark it gives off
the most delicious smell so that I
presume that it's pollinated by
moths. The stem, when
broken gives off the smell
of boiled milk which
I find incongruous
with its heady perfume.
Often it throws up suckers
which can be transplanted in the
early Spring. It grows about ten
foot high and is very attractive
even when in leaf in the Spring.
Summer brings flowers and Autumn
berries, and its Winter shape betrays
its Chinese origin.

SEPTEMBER

There is a touch of Autumn
in the air.   Heleniums, plentifully
covered with miniature sunflowers,
stand four foot high. The centres are
made of brown velvet.   Impossibly
yellow flowers cover the calceolarias
and the Michaelmas daisies are
beginning to come into flower. They
range from blue to purple in every
shade between.   Berry time
is coming.   First to appear are
the seeds of the paeony Black shiny
seeds flanked by vivid red.   The
St John's wort bush has pretty seeds.
They are so shapely.
    I spent the morning cutting back
the Senecio maritima which
has grown quite ungainly and
pulling up yards of convolvulus.
First I put Fison's Evergreen
on the lawn. Concentrating on
the weeds and spreading meanly
on the good turf. But I'll
have to buy another bag.

For me the white Japanese
Anemone (elegans alba) is so much
more beautiful than the pink or red
forms (elegans 'Kriemhilde' and
'Margaret'). These anemones
are so attractive growing about three foot
high and blooming through August and
most of September. Together with the
hydrangeas they are the most colourful
flowers in the garden now. There is not a
lot more out ~ although the buddleias continue to bloom and are attracting
crowds of butterflies.

The Japanese anemones are a
bit weed like in the greediness of
their territorial claims but as hardy
perennials well worth fitting into
a sunny corner where their gusto
for extending themselves will not
become a nuisance.

There is a lovely haze of pink
and white dwarf cyclamen. They
grow everywhere, especially in the churchyard next door. I have a theory

that these delightful flowers may have
been introduced to Bonchurch by Henry de
vere Stacpoole ~ mostly known for his
fashionable novel: "The Blue Lagoon".
He holidayed every year at Bordighera
in Italy and that is where he bought
the handsome wrought iron entrance gates.
    He lived in this house for the last
thirty years of his life.   With care it
is possible to choose varieties that will bloom
both now and in the Spring and Summer.
Their corms are round and smooth at the
bottom and pitted with buds (not roots) at the top. So
be careful not to plant them upside down and
also quite shallowly in well drained soil.
Cyclamen europaeum flowers in the Spring and
early Summer, Coum in Mid Winter to the Spring
and Cilicium in the Autumn.   Again, I prefer
the white ones but these are rarer.
    They seed themselves and soon increase
and multiply if left to their own devices.
They don't like being disturbed. The leaves
come before the flowers and are prettily
marbled. (See p. 16, 17)

There is a large patch of lily like flowers with great strap like leaves. These are about three inches wide and a yard long. They push up in the Spring and have a strange architectural appeal. Then, suddenly in late August or early September they send up great sprouts which open into white flowers with nigger brown anthers. Not much scent but great majesty and beauty. They were here when we first came to live here and I cannot find their name.* So I call them the Victorian lilies. They spread by underground stems and increase yearly. The flowers stand about three foot high. Nearby is a charming shrub called:

* Crinum powellii albu

130

Caryopteris clandonensis which is just coming
into full flowering. It was given to us
as a silver wedding present,
because the back of the leaves
is silver. Also they are pleasantly
aromatic. If you rub your
fingers gently through the leaves
they have a pleasant
herby smell. The
bush grows about
three foot high. In
the Winter it looks
quite dead. Early in the
Spring it should be pruned hard
back. Then, miraculously tiny
buds burgeon out of the seemingly
dead twigs. The aromatic leaves
follow and finally its full glory
is the dainty clusters of blue/mauve
flowers which last for a month to six
weeks. They have a pink hydrangea
beyond them and the colours
contrast attractively with eachother.

131

Sedum spectabile is a generous
plant ~ the one illustrated is
Autumn Joy. I bought one
plant and now I have dozens.
It grows neatly and in the
Spring has beautiful blue/
green fleshy leaves. These
pulled away from the base and
thrust in anywhere will flower
the same year. Once in flower
they attract the bees and the
butterflies. They last almost
for ever as cut flowers, make
roots in the water and, again
can be planted out. They
look particularly good
growing out of crevices
among the rocks.
   Another favourite of mine
is the wild flower Toadflax
(linaria vulgaris) ~ a
type of wild antirrhinum.
   Another success has

been growing geraniums from seed. I bought a packet from Dobies and now I have more than a dozen plants in varying shades. Once again taking cuttings is just too easy. This plant overwintered in a sheltered spot under a south wall and has flowered its head off. The rest I brought indoors and they are far behind ~ but very healthy and all in heavy bud now planted out in a southern bed. To take cuttings, cut beneath a node ~ that is where the leaves come out of the stem. Trim off these leaves and pot up in gritty soil ~ remove any flower buds. They can be grown indoors and planted out in May/June when the frosts have gone, after first hardening them off. They will flower until Christmas. August is the classic month to take cuttings to ensure having more plants ready for next year. It's well worth doing now that plants are so expensive to buy.

These pink lilies
flower in profusion in
the Autumn and like the
Nerines they are naked
of leaves which come
at quite a different
time.   I think
they are Amaryllis
but the first
bulb was given
me by my son when
he was very young and
he treated me to it from his pocket
money.   It was brought at Kingston
Market for 4d and now there are
dozens.   The pink grey
leaves of Rosa rubrifolia are
beautiful for months. Their flowers
are tiny, pink and unimportant
except that they turn into tiny
hips which clash vibrantly
with the charming colour of
the leaves.

134

Vitis henryana is
always beautiful from
early Spring until it
loses its leaves -
but at this time
it surpasses itself,
its leaves blushing to a
fiery crimson. It grows
well on a West wall and
turns a better colour
if it doesn't
have too much direct
sunlight.
I love the hips of the Austrian
briar (p. 93) which are gold and
large and glamourous.
They are prolific and
the climber, now ten
foot high is covered
with them. I think this
is my favourite of the
single roses all of which
I hold in high esteem.

135

The vines are covered in little bunches of grapes and we are too lazy, or busy, to disbud them to get larger fruit. By the end of October, the black one, Black Hamburg, and the white one Chasselas d'Or, get quite ripe and sweet on a good year. But, whatever the weather, in November we harvest them and make a fruit jelly for winter use with mutton and game ~ or with Nursery bread and butter. The secret is not to add any water or they will not set. These vines are now twenty five years old and if not quite as they should be look very pretty and shade the loggia on the south west side of the house. They should be pruned in January and cut back so that each long rod just has a knobbly piece where the side shoots grow in the Spring. If only one bud is allowed to develop from each of these spurs and that is stopped once the flower buds appear much better quality fruit will be forthcoming.

136

Old man's beard or Wild Clematis is another of my favourite weeds. I used to allow it to grow, self-sown, in the garden. But like Topsy it just grew and started to take over in a most greedy and rapacious way. So, with regret, I had to eliminate it. However, it grows wild in all the hedges around and is very beautiful now. To get it to change into really white fluff for use in dried flower arrangements it must be picked now while it is still green. Then it goes pure white. If left it goes a grubby grey.

Out of a hawthorn bush
Tumbled a drunken thrush.
Old man's beard festoons the hedge
Like tinsel on a Christmas tree.
Tall beeches veiled in blue distance
Meet the sky ~
Delight my eye ~

October comes to-morrow and still the field of sunflowers at Newchurch have late blooms coming into their full glory. There is a shortage of blooms now with which to decorate the church for the Harvest Festival. Having picked one sunflower to use in this book I am delighted to find that it is very happy in a vase and showing no sign of fading. So this afternoon I'm going to pick a lot so that they can shine in the dark corners of the church.

One of the rock plants which really is at its best at this late season is Zauschneria cana ~ I wish it had a common name ~ no wonder I had to look it up! It grows into a very large cushion about a foot high and goes on flowering for some weeks. It looks good with the dwarf Michaelmas daisies. These are another of my difficulties. With the help of the bees they keep on begetting giant children. For three years I have dug these monsters up and put them elsewhere. They seldom thrive but the bit left behind grows into a sturdy plant. I have given them best. If giants wish to grow in shallow soil on top of a rock, why thwart them?

OCTOBER

October has come in accompanied by force eight
gales and torrential rain.   Now and then there
are a few hours of sunshine and in its Autumnal
shafts the serried ranks of the Lords and Ladies
shine like orange sentinels.   They are the
showiest thing in the garden ~ the fruits of
Arum maculatum.   I love their flowers in
the Spring (p. 71) and their showy berries
are an added bonus.

The pink colour of the elderberry leaves is
another sign that Autumn is here. So is the
flowering of the Autumn crocus (Colchicum
speciosum).   Their corms should be planted
in August.   Their beauty is enhanced by
the way the flowers thrust naked through the
grass and open their starlike flowers. Later they
have not very attractive coarse leaves. These
must be left uncut if you want them to
flower again the next year. So they are best
naturalised in rough grass that does not
mind being left uncut until late June.
They last well in water and close and
reopen as the light shines upon them.

The seed heads of the Montbretia are quite attractive and make a good background for Winter flower arrangements.

I find Montbretia need the most drastic thinning and at this time it is good to dig up the large clumps and return only the best and fattest corms. These planted four inches apart ensure blooms for next year and not outsize tussocks of "grass." If the clumps have been really neglected strings of "necklaces" of corms can be found ~ rather like "pop~it" beads ~~ The nasturtiums have been flowering for months and are still making a good

how.   They seem to rejoice in poor
gritty soil.   The young leaves
roughly chopped and well seasoned
with sea salt and freshly ground
black pepper make delicious
sandwiches spread between well buttered
wholemeal bread.   They
are also good chopped
and mixed with yogurt
as a winter relish
or a side-dish with curry.
African Marigolds
are another annual
that really does
give value for money.
They flower for months
and last
very
well
in water
as a
cut
flower.

143

Berries tumble from the sky. Most colour now
is in the hedgerows. Rowan trees are loden with
fruit ~ although last night's gale has turned the
pavement pink, strewn with fallen yew berries. Although
the yew has such a bad name for being poisonous the
berries taste very nice ~ all one has to do is not to bite
the centre and be sure to spit it out having sucked
off the outside sweetness. The birds agree with me ~
especially the thrushes. I love Yew trees and the
golden form: Taxus fastigiata aurea makes a slow
growing handsome shrub in the garden giving a

144

golden glow beside darker evergreens.

Blackberries are still ripening and their pink flowers in Summer and pretty fruits in Autumn end up with the leaves turning the most glorious colours. My mother made beautiful arrangements of these leaves displayed in an earthenware pitcher with a white washed wall for background. It is possible to plant a thornless variety in the garden and this is a vigorous grower and producer if planted in rich soil with a sunny aspect.

My three year old granddaughter calls them: "Black belties" ~ which they will always be for me now ~~

There is one thing about the weather. My September sewn grass seed is growing quite wonderfully.

Outdoor single Chrysanthemums are
making a pleasing show now. They
are very hardy and the easiest plants
I know to take cuttings from.   In the
Spring when they first start to show
growth, heeled cuttings can be cut away from
the main stool. Use a sharp knife and
plant them where they are going to
flower. All they need is a little
sharp sand or grit put into the
place where they are to be rooted.
about a handful for each cutting.
Later when the shoots are more
developed I like to pinch out a
lot of growth to keep the plants
shapely and to encourage more flowers.
not just a few at the top of long spikes.
Each of these cuttings can be rooted by
cutting immediately under a joint and
taking off the two bottom leaves.
     The single flowers come in many
colours: maroon, red, copper, yellow, pink
and mauve in various shades. They all
have bright yellow centres ~ sometimes a greeny

146

yellow.   They make excellent cut
flowers which last well in water.
All the cottages in this village have
them.   Without much colour about they
make a very useful contribution.
        The seeds of the stinking iris: Iris
foetida (the flower is illustrated on
page 96) have now popped open
revealing their bright coral berries
which stay on for a long time.   Once
they start to split they may be
brought indoors to brighten up winter arrangements of dried grasses
and bracken ~ the latter dries well
under the carpet.   The plants are easy
to raise from seed.   The berries stay bright
well into January and February.
        If privet is not clipped ~ sometimes it
can. be found growing wild in hedge rows ~
it displays handsome spikes of jet black
berries.   These look very well mixed with
the orange of the iris seeds.   Another
pleasing colour is the dark red shoots of our
wild Dogwood which may be gathered once

147

the leaves have dropped.

Ivy is now well in flower. I find this a puzzling creeper. The usual wild ivy we all know so well eventually reaches the top of a wall or a tree and changes its nature. It sends up strong stems with quite different shaped leaves which support their round heads of green florets with yellow stamens. I was surprised how strong the smell was once the flower was in my studio. What pollinates them at this time of the year? The leaves are very shiny and reflect any Autumn sunshine. They last in water for simply ages and look attractive mixed with the bright iris berries.

I like to go round now searching for next year's promise. The catkins of Garrya elliptica ~ illustrated on page 26 ~ are thickly present all over the bush ~ silver grey against the very, dark evergreen leaves.   In themselves, even at this stage, they make an attractive display.

The mimosa tree for the first time is smothered with flower buds and before long in late January or early February we shall be dazzled with their golden fluffy heads and the sweetness of their smell.

Camellias have fat buds of promise too. They enjoy this very wet weather but a lot of the garden is disappointing and bedraggled.

I can never understand why grass so much prefers growing in the flower beds to its proper place on the lawn! I am delighted that the newly sown grass has done so well in the lawn but I am wondering if it would have done just as well had I prepared the soil and sown nothing? It's so wet under foot that it is going to be difficult to weed it out of the flower beds which I had hoped were weed free ~~

149

I'm still waiting optimistically
for a St. Martin's Summer. Yesterday was fine but to-day we are back
to a force 9 gale with a force 10
imminent. I think it has arrived!
The salt soaked air is burning the
leaves. In spite of this
gloom the dahlias are still
in flower. The white pom-
poms are very beautiful.
This clump over-
wintered last year in
the good earth and has
been in flower for months.
The Nerines ~ or Naked
Ladies ~ very late this year,
are in full flower. How
bright they are and what
wonderful cut flowers, giving
about three weeks of pleasure
in a vase. Once established
they come up year after year
in ever increasing numbers.
A very useful climber that has been

decorating an ugly fence
for months is Solanum
jasminoides.   This
is still flowering away and
its white bunches are tossing
about in the gale.
    It is quick growing
and very easy to establish.
~ one of the best climbers
for covering an eyesore as
it is not invasive.

151

NOVEMBER

My studio is full of fallen leaves. I cut them in their freshness and very soon they have floated down to the floor, faded, crisped up and quietly died. This is the season of carmine and gold leaves which burst into colour and then demurely disappear until I wonder if my paints have exaggerated the exuberance of their dying glamour.

Acer purpurea was almost the same colour in the Summer. flowering cherry leaves turn the most amazing yellow and show off the plum colour of the Winter flowering Prunus cerasifera 'Atropurpurea ~ the Purple leaved Plum.

Hydrangea hortensia 'Hamburg' goes glowing carmine in the Autumn.

I call it Winter flowering because the flowers follow fast after leaf drop.

153

Ginko biloba ~ the Maidenhair tree ~ older than time and a throw-back to pre-history is a very beautiful tree. Now it has turned clear yellow and against the clear blue sky is very handsome.

Acer campestre, our own native Field Maple, turns an equally attractive yellow. Once they were rivalled by the yellow leaves of the elms. I always meant to paint them against an angry grey sky with shafts of sunlight enhancing their gold. But they are all dead and felled and now I shall never be able to try to record their beauty.

Root saplings are growing and a few are turning yellow. I wonder if they will ever grow into forest trees? So far the few that have grown into small trees have succomed to the dread disease.

My front door faces due North. I have two large wooden tubs either side in which are two topiary yaffles ~ Lonicera nitida ~ not the most suitable choice as they need frequent haircuts to keep them in shape. Here I put cuttings ~ usually filched ~ and everyday I water them with cold tea. I have a bucket in the kitchen in which I pour all the leftover tea. This method has been most successful and I have rooted hydrangeas, St. John's wort, Hebe, Myrtle and Buddleia this way. The time of year doesn't seem to matter very much although July and August, of course, are the best months.

I'm not very fond of the Hebes, but there is no doubt that they are flowering now and have been for months. There are many colours to choose from and they seed themselves. The trouble is that seedlings have to be allowed to flower to see if they are any good. There are so many wishy~washy ones. There is a robust navy blue strain in our village and a deep magenta. Cuttings are easy to root. As a tribe the Hebes are tender. They come from New Zealand. Even after frost, usually they spring again from bare grey trunks. They grow about four foot high and are bushy and almost evergreen ~ unless frost cuts down their growth. The dry seed heads can be sprayed with gold, silver or bronze paint and used as a Christmas decoration. They are amusing for a week or so ~ but how I enjoy

burning them once twelfth night
has arrived!

Sprays of Schizostylis
coccinea or Crimson Flag, a late
flowering bulbous plant from
South Africa, are looking quite
splendid in the dying garden.
They seem to be perfectly happy if
naturalised in a sheltered spot. Perhaps one of their chief charms is
the unexpectedness of pink lily-like
flowers in November.

This journal was started on 1st January. Now
I'm hoist on my own petard. I have a bunch
of seasonal flowers in my sitting room ~ the pink
crimson flag, golden Jasmine nudiflorum (p. 13)
and Iris stylosa (p. 13). I put them into the
first pages of January, but they are out now
and will flower most of the Winter.

In between the gales the late sunshine still
shows a good deal of colour in leaves and
berries. Deep red leaves of Cotoneaster
horizontalis ~ I wish it had a common name ~
are very showy. The birds have eaten

most of their berries although there are still a few left.
One of the pleasures of Cotoneaster horizontalis is that
it flowers very early in the year and encourages the
first bees.   I love to listen to them in early March
working away at these flowers.   This shrub grows as
its name suggests quite flat and horizontal to walls
and will thrive equally well in a north, south, east or
west position.   It grows very tidily and needs no
staking.   It can be pruned savagely without taking
umbrage and is altogether good natured and attractive.
It is at its best now glowing a deep red against
the grey rocks of the cliff.
          My favourite forest tree, the Beech,
Fagus sylvatica, is the last to open its slender

buds in the Spring. The bonus is
that it is also the last to lose its leaves in the
Autumn. The tree is alight with golden orange
leaves. The trees that I prune and keep as rockery
specimens hold their golden brown leaves until the
Spring. These rockery shrubs are self sown into
crevices and consequently are natural dwarves. I
cut the leading shoot down yearly and the treelets
keep small and trim and are a constant joy in the
depth of Winter.

As the last days of November go on their relent-
less way I am amazed at the colour still to be found
in the gardens and the hedgerows. Berberis is
very good value as a shrub. Its thorns make it
useful as a hedging shrub. There are many varieties:
Berberis darwinii has brilliant orange flowers

in the early spring followed by blue berries. The leaves are small and very shiny. The shrub will eventually grow up to about ten foot but it is a slow grower. Mine is a delight when its orange yellow flowers dazzle the eye against the grey cliff. It is very large and very old.

Now Berberis thunbergii has scarlet berries in profusion and reddish brown leaves. The prickles are long and sharp and a warm light red. Berberis thunbergii erecta is the best variety for hedging as it grows more upright and makes an impenetrable barrier spectacular when in flower and with good berries and leaf colour now.

The Common Spindle Tree, Euonymus europaeus, is another delight. The deciduous leaves turn a charming pink. The fruits are very showy. They are a most

160

vivid pink difficult to represent with water colour and the capsules crack open to show the clashing orange seeds within.

DECEMBER

The twelfth month
is here.   The trees
are bare but the
evergreens make a
          shining show
The brightest
colour in the garden
is the strawberry tree,
Arbutus unedo and the
golden leaves of the Elaeagnus
     pungens compliment it
Red hips glow on the thorny
twigs of our wild roses.

There are many
     attractive evergreens.
So many different shades
of green with an occasional
splash of gold to brighten
everything up. In a
small garden it is diff-
icult to fit in all of
these but even so
there are small
evergreen subjects which

163

can be used to
brighten up the
Winter months.

Griselinia littoralis 'Raoul'
can be kept quite small and tidy and will
make an excellent hedge, especially if you
live near the sea.   I have never seen its
pale apple coloured fleshy leaves spoiled by
salt spray.   Its golden variety: G. variegata is very
effective and I like to see the two grown together.
     They come from New Zealand and are apt to be
prone to frost in inland areas.   It is curious how
the sea, which spoils so many plants with its salt
spray when there is a gale, can help to save delicate
subjects from the risk of frosts.   I suppose it is just

a matter of
growing what is happy
in our own neighbourhood.   Still it is very
tempting to try to succeed with something a
little different.   My Mother was a very
knowledgeable gardener and I remember one
day being amused when she said impatiently:
"I'm tired of convalescents in my garden!" As
I grow older I understand what she meant ~~
      Another golden subject is the conifer
Chamaecyparis lawsoniana 'Ellwood's Gold'. Often these
are grown as hedges, which I find overpowering, but a
single bush growing out of a green lawn adds a glow to
December.
      The showy hips on bare bush roses also cheer
this month. Most of these roses have bright bunches
of hips irrespective of variety and should not be

dead-headed
until you Know
which carry colour
through the Winter.
I am amazed how
much colour the stems of bare
willows display, livid yellow, green
and red.   This one: Salix alba
'Vitellina' is very yellow to-day and
I see in Hilliers Manual of Trees they
say it needs to be pruned severely every other year
to maintain its 'yolk-of-egg' colour.
Another display comes from the crab apple: Malus
'Golden Hornet' which Keeps its fruits late into the
end and, indeed, the beginning of the year.   It has a

neat habit of growth and charming
flowers in the early Summer.

The ordinary golden privet needs to
be grown as a free standing shrub to appreciate
its beauty.   Uncut by shears its twigs have very
attractive habits and the colour is vibrant.

The shrub rose Rosa moyesii is now bare except
for a few golden bud tops of leaves and the last of the
orange hips.   It makes a beautiful hedge and the
colour, although nearly gone is still eye-catching.

It is quite wonderful how much colour is still to
be found and I find some of my most **success ful**
flower arrangements come from these twigs and
berries, golden evergreen bushes and bare branches
and fruits.   Dried hydrangea flowers are very
useful and go the most artistic shades.

The berries of the Pyracanthus
or Firethorn are a fiery
orange on the wall.   In
a neighbour's garden
higher up the cliff which
catches more frost than
we do the carmine red
leaves of the Mahonia
japonica (see page 20)
are spectacular.

   Ours are in flower and
smell very sweet but the leaves
are green.

   I've just been given a garden gift token for
Christmas and I hope it will buy me the beautiful
ivy: Hedera "Buttercup." The leaves go a pure
golden yellow if grown in full sun and I have just
the place for it on a southern wall of cliff.

   And so the year draws to its close - but it
isn't the end - just a new beginning.   The
daffodil tips are thrusting through the thawed
earth, a few roses continue foolishly to bud

and open into rather
tattered blooms, the Jasmine
nudiflorum is joyful with yellow
flowers and the budding mimosa looks yellower each
day.

Spring is the next attraction. How difficult it is
to be patient, but it will come and burst forth once
again into the glory of the garden and the cycle of the
year.

Yaffles, Bonchurch, 31st December 1981

173

31. 12. 1981

Yaffles garden before